بسم الله الرحمن الرحيم

We begin with the name of Allāh,
the Most Merciful, the Ever Merciful

The First Steps
IN PRACTISING ISLAM

The First Steps
IN PRACTISING ISLAM

Compiled by
Shaykh Omar Subedar

Mathabah

ISBN 978-1511713627
First Edition

Author	Omar Subedar
Editor	Ibrahim Baig
Scholarly review	Mufti Ibrahim Kureshi, Academy of Research in Islamic Jurisprudence (ARIJ), (www.arij.ca)
Cover designer	Umair Irfan
Arabic typing	Omar Subedar
Design & Typesetting	ARM (www.whitethreadpress.com)

Contents

Belief (*Īmān*)

Legal (*Fiqh*) Terms

Purification

TRANSLITERATION TABLE

ء (أ إ) ' (A slight catch in the breath. It is also used to indicate where the *hamza* has been dropped from the beginning of a word.)

ا a, ā

ب b

ت t

ث th (Should be pronounced as the *th* in *thin* or *thirst*.)

ج j

ح ḥ (Tensely breathed *h* sound.)

خ kh (Pronounced like the *ch* in Scottish *loch* with the mouth hollowed to produce a full sound.)

د d

ذ dh (Should be pronounced as the *th* in *this* or *that*.)

ر r

ز z

س s

ش sh

ص ṣ (A heavy *s* pronounced far back in the mouth with the mouth hollowed to produce a full sound.)

ض ḍ (A heavy *d/dh* pronounced far back in the mouth with the mouth hollowed to produce a full sound.)

ط ṭ (A heavy *t* pronounced far back in the mouth with the mouth hollowed to produce a full sound.)

ظ ẓ (A heavy *dh* pronounced far back in the mouth with the mouth hollowed to produce a full sound.)

ع ʿ, ʿa, ʿi, ʿu (Pronounced from the throat.)

غ gh (Pronounced like a throaty French *r* with the mouth hollowed to produce a full sound.)

ف f

ق q (A guttural *q* sound with the mouth hollowed to produce a full sound.)

ك k

ل l

م m

ن n

و w, ū, u.

ه h

ي y, ī, i

Preface

All praise is for Allāh ﷻ who has blessed us with Islam. We would not have been guided had Allāh ﷻ not guided us. We pray to Allāh ﷻ to continuously shower His blessings and mercy upon His final and noblest messenger to humanity, Muḥammad ibn ʿAbdullāh ﷺ.

Islam is a religion that has gained tremendous international attention in recent times. It is a pragmatic way of life offering real solutions to the trials we face every day. It is a religion that is lived, and not simply a collection of abstract concepts that is up for discussion and debate in lecture halls and living rooms. It has been tried, tested and proven successful in bringing about positive reform in societies where it was embraced.

Living as a Muslim minority in a secular society comes with its challenges. Every so often we run into a situation where there is a conflict of values. We ultimately are made to choose between the status quo to maintain our social acceptance or to defy it and be reduced to a social outcast. This puts a great strain on many Muslim Westerners thus leaving them to question the relevance of Islam in the 21st century. This questioning leads a number of them to look deeper into their religion and conclude for themselves whether they see value in giving this lifestyle preference or not.

Thus they take advantage of every opportunity they are afforded to learn about Islam, whether it be reading articles on the internet, taking online or in-class courses, or going to a retreat for a duration of time. During this pursuit many are left to wonder where to begin their studies from as they become exposed to the sheer vastness and depth of the religion. People end up taking courses or reading material that is far ahead of their current comprehension of Islam thus leaving them even more confused than before.

Undoubtedly, seeking knowledge of Islam is a duty for every Muslim.[1] However just like in any field of study, Islam is to be learnt in a structured manner. This is understood from the instructions our beloved Prophet ﷺ issued Muʿādh ibn Jabal ؓ when deploying him to govern Yemen: "You are going to a community of [people who are the] 'People of the Scripture' (*Ahl al-Kitāb*). When you reach them, invite them to testify that there is no god besides Allāh and Muḥammad is the Messenger of Allāh. If they listen to you then tell them that Allāh has ordained five ritual prayers on them for every morning and evening. If they listen to you then tell them that Allāh has made a payment necessary for them which will be taken from their affluent and given to their needy [. . .]."[2]

Structured learning always guarantees optimum results. It is for this reason Mathabah Publications has decided to make a contribution in the field of Islamic studies by presenting this book, The First Steps in Practising Islam.

This book has been prepared to serve as an introductory book for those who wish to learn the essential aspects of Islam and for those who intend to pursue higher Islamic studies in the areas of creed and ritual worship. With the convenience of the reader in mind, this book has been structured in bullet points while being

1 *Sunan Ibn Mājah* 224

2 *Ṣaḥīḥ al-Bukhārī* 1496

supplemented with a source for almost every point, thus addressing the what, how and why. Citing sources from the Qurʿān and *ḥadīth* was of paramount importance when preparing this book. It is imperative for Muslims to be connected with Islamic scripture as much as possible, for this is the only way they can develop insight and confidence in their religion.

This book comprises of the most fundamental and important aspects of Islamic beliefs (*ʿaqīdah*), purification (*ṭahārah*), ritual prayer (*ṣalāh*), wealth purification (*zakāh*) and fasting (*ṣawm*). Key discussions were carefully identified with the criteria of immediate practical usefulness and relevance. Plain English was adopted to relay the information so that the scope of its benefit could be as broad as possible. It is to this end that literal translations of the Qurʿān and *ḥadīth* texts have been largely avoided in favour of contextual ones. All *fiqh* rulings are in accordance to the Ḥanafī School of Islamic Law.

This book has been concluded with a section on essential traits every Muslim is required to adopt in order to remain spiritually healthy. Experience dictates that when a person becomes immersed in learning the technicalities of the Islam, he loses sight of the real objective of the religion, which is to practise Islam to please Allāh ﷻ. Learning the intricate details of Islamic practices and developing good Islamic behaviour go hand in hand; they are inseparable. The moment one is pursued in the absence of the other a great spiritual imbalance materializes.

We pray to Allāh ﷻ that He accepts this humble endeavour and make it a source of benefit for generations to come. Āmīn.

Omar Subedar
Toronto, Ontario.
February 18, 2014

About the Author

Mohammed Omar Subedar was born in 1977 and grew up in the Greater Toronto Area, Canada. In 1990, he enrolled in the Institute of Islamic Education in Dewsbury, United Kingdom, where in 1993 he became a *ḥafiẓ* of the Qur'ān. In 2001 he graduated from the same institute with the title of Scholar of Islamic Sciences and Arabic Literature, earning a final grade of A. This seven-year program covered:

- Arabic grammar (*naḥw*), morphology (*ṣarf*), rhetoric (*balāghah*), vocabulary and literature
- Islamic creed (*ʿaqīdah*)
- Exegesis (*tafsīr*) of the Qur'ān and principles (*uṣūl*) of exegesis
- Islamic law (*fiqh*) according to the Ḥanafī school (*madh'hab*)
- Comparative studies of the four schools of Islamic law (Ḥanafī, Shāfiʿī, Mālikī and Ḥanbalī) and principles of jurisprudence (*uṣūl al-fiqh*)

- Prophetic traditions (*aḥādīth*) and the principles (*uṣūl*) of *ḥadīth* studies
- Islamic history
- Pronunciation of the Qur'ān (*tajwīd*) according to the 10 major styles of recitation (*qira'āt*)

Since 2011, Mohammed Omar Subedar has been a lecturer on *ḥadīth* literature at the Islamic Society of Peel. Among the books he has taught are:

- *Mu'aṭṭa' li-Imām Muḥammad*
- *Mu'aṭṭa' li-Imām Mālik*
- *Sunan Abū Dāwūd*
- *Jāmi' al-Tirmidhī*
- *Ṣaḥīḥ al-Bukhārī*
- *Ṣaḥīḥ Muslim*

Currently he is the Dean of the Mathabah Institute, the CEO of Bukhari Publications, the COO of the Halal Monitoring Authority, and an imam at the Islamic Society of Peel.

Belief

(*Īmān*)

BELIEF (*ĪMĀN*)

God's (Allāh's) message to humanity

People, the Messenger (Muḥammad ﷺ) has come to you with the truth from your Lord, so believe; it is better for you. But if you disbelieve [in it], then indeed Allāh owns everything in the heavens and the earth. And Allāh is ever Knowing and Wise.[3]

Indeed, those who have said, "Our Lord is Allāh," and then remained steadfast [on the right course]—the angels will descend upon them saying, "Do not fear and do not be upset, but [rather] receive the good news of the Paradise you were promised. We [angels] were your allies in the worldly life and are so in the Hereafter. And you will have in [Paradise] whatever your souls desire and there you will have whatever you request as hospitality from a Master who is Forgiving and Merciful."[4]

3 Sūrat al-Nisā' 4:171

4 Sūrat al-Fuṣṣilat 41:30–32

WHAT IS ĪMĀN?

Allāh's Messenger, Muḥammad ﷺ said, "*Īmān* is to believe in:

- Allāh
- His angels
- His scriptures
- His messengers
- the Last Day
- and to believe in destiny, [both] the favourable and unfavourable [parts] of it."[5]

WHAT ARE MY BELIEFS IN ALLĀH ﷻ?

- Allāh ﷻ is the only divine being in existence.[6] Of all the world religions, Islam is the only one that believes that divinity is completely reserved for Allāh ﷻ.
- Assigning divinity to a person or an object, or to consider something equal to Allāh ﷻ is called *shirk*; a sin that Allāh ﷻ will never forgive on the Day of Judgement.[7]

5 *Ṣaḥīḥ Muslim* 93

6 "Say, 'He, Allāh, is One'" (Sūrat al-Ikhlāṣ 112:1)

"And your God is one God. There is no divine being except Him, the Entirely Merciful, the Especially Merciful." (Sūrat al-Baqarah 2:163)

"Had there been gods in the heavens and earth besides Allāh, the heavens and earth would have been ruined [. . .]" (Sūrat al-Anbiyā' 21:22)

7 "Without a doubt, Allāh will not forgive [that others be] associated with Him [in divinity], but He will forgive whoever He likes for what is less than [the sin of shirk]. And those who associate others with Allāh [in divinity] have certainly gone far off track." (Sūrat al-Nisā' 4: 116)

- Nothing resembles Allāh ﷻ,[8] and nothing is equal to Allāh ﷻ.[9] Allāh ﷻ is genderless and Allāh's essence is beyond our comprehension.[10]
- Allāh ﷻ is independent of the creation[11] while the entire creation is dependent on Allāh ﷻ.[12]
- Allāh ﷻ is the sole creator of everything.[13]
- Allāh ﷻ alone gives sustenance to His entire creation.[14]
- Worship is solely reserved for Allāh ﷻ, and assistance is to be sought only from Him.[15]
- Allāh ﷻ is characterized by attributes of perfection and is free of all deficiencies. Hence:

Anas ﷺ reported, "I was told that the Prophet ﷺ said to Muʿādh ﷺ, "Whoever meets Allāh without having associated partners with Him will enter Paradise." [. . .] (*Ṣaḥīḥ al-Bukhārī* 128)

8 "There is nothing like His resemblance [. . .]." (Sūrat al-Shūrā 42:11)

9 "And no one is equal to Him." (Sūrat al-Ikhlāṣ 112:4)

10 "So do not present examples of Allāh. Indeed, Allāh knows while you do not know." (Sūrat al-Naḥl 16:74)

11 "Allāh is free of need, while you are in need [of Him] [. . .]." (Sūrat Muḥammad 47:38)

12 "People, you are in need of Allāh, while Allāh the Praiseworthy is free of need. If He wills, He can do away with you and bring forth a new creation. This is not difficult for Allāh." (Sūrat al-Fāṭir 35:15–17)

13 "Allāh is the Creator of all things and He is in charge of everything." (Sūrat al-Zumar 39:62)

14 "Indeed, it is Allāh who is the continuous Provider, the firm Possessor of strength." (Sūrat al-Dhāriyāt 51:58)

15 "It is You [Allāh] we worship and You [Allāh] we ask for help." (Sūrat al-Fātiḥah 1:5)

"People, worship your Master, who created you and those before you, so that you may become righteous." (Sūrat al-Baqarah 2:21)

(1) Allāh ﷻ is alive and will never die.[16]

(2) Allāh ﷻ has no beginning and no end.[17]

(3) Allāh ﷻ is the All-Powerful and is weakened by nothing.[18]

(4) Allāh's knowledge is absolute. He never forgets.[19]

(5) Allāh ﷻ hears all and sees all.[20]

(6) Allāh ﷻ speaks to whomsoever He likes, such as His messengers.[21] When speaking about Himself He often refers to Himself with the 'royal We' in the sacred texts.

◇ Allāh ﷻ does as He pleases and is accountable to none.[22]

---

16 "And rely upon the Ever-Living [Allāh] who will not die, and exalt Allāh with His praise." (Sūrat al-Furqān 25:58)

17 "He neither gives birth nor is He born." (Sūrat al-Ikhlāṣ 112:3)

"He is the First and the Last." (Sūrat al-Ḥadīd 57:3)

18 "He is competent over all things." (Sūrat al-Ḥadīd 57:2)

"He is neither overcome by drowsiness nor sleep." (Sūrat al-Baqarah 2:255)

"[. . .] but if you choose to turn away [from Allāh] then know that you will not make Allāh fail." (Sūrat al-Tawbah 9:3)

19 "[. . .] and know that Allāh is Knowing of all things." (Sūrat al-Baqarah 2:231)

"He knows what is before them and what will be after them, and they do not encompass a thing of His knowledge except for what He wills." (Sūrat al-Baqarah 2:255)

"My Master neither errs nor does He forget." (Sūrat Ṭāhā 20:52)

20 "Indeed, Allāh is Hearing and Seeing." (Sūrat al-Ḥajj 22:75)

21 "These messengers; We have given superiority to some of them over others [among them]. There were those among them who Allāh spoke to directly, and He raised some of them in ranks. (Sūrat al-Baqarah 2:253)

22 "He continuously puts into effect whatever He intends." (Sūrat al-Burūj 85:16)

"Indeed, Allāh does as He wills." (Sūrat al-Ḥajj 22:18)

"He is not questioned about what He does, but they [the people] will be questioned." (Sūrat al-Anbiyā᾿ 21:23)

WHAT ARE MY BELIEFS IN THE ANGELS?

- Angels are a creation of Allāh ﷻ. They have been created from light.[23]
- Angels are the noble servants of Allāh ﷻ.[24]
- Angels always carry out Allāh's orders and never disobey Him.[25]
- The tasks assigned to angels involve:
  - (1) Glorifying Allāh ﷻ and prostrating to Him.[26]
  - (2) Praying for the Prophet Muḥammad ﷺ[27] and the believers (*mu'minūn*).[28]
  - (3) Conveying Allāh's messages[29] and passing along revelation.[30]

---

23 ʿĀ'ishah ؓ reported, "Allāh's Messenger ﷺ said, 'The Angels were created from light [. . .].'" (*Ṣaḥīḥ Muslim* 7495)

24 "[. . .] rather they are honoured servants." (Sūrat al-Anbiyā' 21:26)

25 "[. . .] they do not disobey Allāh in what He commands them [to do]; rather they do as they are told." (Sūrat al-Taḥrīm 66:6)

26 "Indeed, those who are near your Master are not prevented by arrogance from His worship. They exalt Him, and prostrate to Him." (Sūrat al-Aʿrāf 7:206)

27 "Indeed, Allāh grants blessings to the Prophet, and His angels invoke Allāh to do so." (Sūrat al-Aḥzāb 33:56)

28 "Those [angels] who carry the Throne and the [angels] around it engage in glorifying [Allāh] with the praises of their Sustainer; they believe in Him and ask forgiveness for the believers, saying, 'Our Master, You have covered all things in [Your] mercy and knowledge, so forgive those who have repented and followed Your way, and protect them from the punishment of the blazing fire." (Sūrat al-Ghāfir 40:7)

29 "Allāh chooses messengers from the angels [. . .]." (Sūrat al-Ḥajj 22:75)

30 "And indeed, [the Qur'ān] is revelation from the Sustainer of the worlds. The trustworthy spirit (Jibrīl) brought it down upon your heart, [Muḥammad, so] that you may be a warner." (Sūrat al-Shuʿarā' 26:192–194)

(4) Guarding humans and recording their deeds.[31]

WHAT ARE MY BELIEFS IN THE SCRIPTURES?

◇ Every scripture that a messenger (*rasūl*) passed to his nation was revelation from Allāh 🌸. These scriptures were never authored nor composed by the messengers themselves.[32]

◇ Allāh sent four main scriptures:

(1) The Tawrāt to Mūsā 🌸.[33]

(2) The Zabūr to Dāwūd 🌸.[34]

(3) The Injīl to ʿĪsā 🌸.[35]

(4) The Qurʾān to Muḥammad 🌸.[36]

◇ Allāh 🌸 also sent other scriptures to other messengers.[37]

---

31 "And indeed, protectors are appointed over you who are noble and are recording. They know everything you do." (Sūrat al-Infiṭār 82:10–12)

32 "Nor does he (Muḥammad) speak from [his own] inclination. [The Qurʾān] is simply revelation revealed [by Allāh]." (Sūrat al-Najm 53:3–4)

33 "[And remember] when We gave Mūsā the scripture and criterion so that you would possibly become guided." (Sūrat al-Baqarah 2:53)

"Indeed, We sent down the Tawrāt, in which there was guidance and light." (Sūrat al-Māʾidah 5:44)

34 "[. . .] and We gave the Zabūr to Dāwūd." (Sūrat al-Nisāʾ 4:163)

35 "And We sent ʿĪsā, the son of Maryam, in their footsteps, to confirm the Tawrāt that had been sent before him. And We gave him the Injīl, in which there was guidance and light, and confirmation of the previous book i.e. the Tawrāt. [We sent it] as guidance and instruction for the righteous." (Sūrat al-Māʾidah 5:46)

36 "And hence We revealed an Arabic Qurʾān to you so that you may [use it to] warn the Mother of Cities (i.e. Makkah) and those around it, and warn [everyone] of the Day of Assembly, about which there is no doubt." (Sūrat al-Shūrā 42:7)

37 "Undoubtedly, this is in the former scriptures; the scriptures of Ibrāhīm and

---

- Previous scriptures have been altered throughout time.[38] The Qur'ān on the other hand has always remained under Allāh's protection. It has been preserved word for word from the time of its revelation.[39]

- The Qur'ān is Allāh's word[40] and has been revealed for the guidance of humanity.[41]

- The Qur'ān is not the word of a human being. Whosoever claims it is has been challenged to produce literature that is comparable to it.[42]

- The Qur'ān was revealed in its entirety from the protected tablets to the first heaven.[43] From the first heaven it was sent down in portions over a span of 23 years to the Messenger ﷺ as the need arose.[44]

Mūsā." (Sūrat al-Aʿlā 87:18–19)

38 "Among the Jews are those who alter words from their proper usages [. . .]." (Sūrat al-Nisā' 4:46)

"They alter words from their proper usages and have forgotten a portion of what they were reminded of." (Sūrat al-Mā'idah 5:13)

39 "Without doubt, it is We who sent down the Qur'ān and indeed, We will protect it." (Sūrat al-Ḥijr 15:9)

40 "And without a doubt, the Qur'ān is the revelation of the Sustainer of the worlds." (Sūrat al-Shuʿrā' 26:192)

41 "Undoubtedly, this Qur'ān guides [people] to what is most suitable [to follow in life] and congratulates the believers who do good deeds that they will have a great reward. And those who do not believe in the Hereafter—We have prepared for them a painful punishment." (Sūrat al-Isrā' 17:9–10)

42 "And if you are in doubt over what We have revealed to Our servant [Muḥammad], then produce a chapter (sūrah) similar to it. And call upon your witnesses, other than Allāh, if you are truthful. But if you do not [produce something similar to it], and you never will be able to, then fear the fire [of Hell], whose fuel is men and stones. It has been prepared for the disbelievers." (Sūrat al-Baqarah 2:23–24)

43 "Indeed, We sent the Qur'ān down on the Night of Decree." (Sūrat al-Qadr 97:1)

44 "[And it is] a Qur'ān, which We have separated into portions so that you

- The Qur'ān is a book of absolute perfection and is free of any defects.[45]
- The believer must recite it,[46] ponder over it[47] and practise its message.

WHAT ARE MY BELIEFS IN ALLĀH'S MESSENGERS?

- A messenger (*rasūl*) is a human being who has been honoured by Allāh ﷻ with divine revelation (*waḥy*). He is instructed by Allāh ﷻ to convey Allāh's law (*sharīʿah*) to a person or a group of people.[48]
- Allāh ﷻ sent messengers throughout the past to give the good news of Paradise (*Jannah*) to the righteous and to warn the sinful about Hell (*Jahannam*).[49]
- Messengers were all honourable men and were all guided by Allāh ﷻ. It is their direction we must follow and their instructions we must obey.[50]

---

may recite it to people over a prolonged period. And We have sent it down gradually." (Sūrat al-Isrā' 17:106)

45 "[This scripture is] an Arabic Qur'ān, without any crookedness, so that [your community] may become righteous." (Sūrat al-Zumar 39:28)

46 "[. . .] so recite from the Qur'ān whatever is easy for you." (Sūrat al-Muzzammil 73:20)

47 "So do they not reflect over the Qur'ān? If it had been from [a source] other than Allāh, they would have found many contradictions in it." (Sūrat al-Nisā' 4:82)

48 "Their messengers said to them, 'We are only men like you, but Allāh favours whoever He likes from among His servants.'" (Sūrat Ibrāhīm 14:11)

"Tell [them, Messenger], 'I am only a man like you, to whom it has been revealed that your God is one God. So whoever hopes to meet their Master should do good work and not associate anyone in the worship of their Master.'" (Sūrat al-Kahf 18:110)

49 "And We send messengers simply as conveyers of good news, and as warners." (Sūrat al-Anʿām 6:48)

50 "And We gave Is'ḥāq and Yaʿqūb to Ibrāhīm. We guided each one of them.

- Each messenger provided their community with clear signs and miracles to validate their claim to prophethood. These miracles were conferred upon them by Allāh ﷻ. No messenger was ever able to produce miracles on their own.[51]
- Allāh ﷻ has made certain messengers superior to other messengers.[52]
- We do not know the exact number of messengers with certainty.[53]

And before [them] we guided Nūḥ, and among Nūḥ's descendants [we guided] Dāwūd, Sulaymān, Ayyūb, Yūsuf, Mūsā and Hārūn. We compensate those who do well in this manner. And [we guided] Zakarīyā, Yaḥyā, ʿĪsā and Ilyās; each one [them] was from the righteous. And [we guided] Ismāʿīl, Alyasaʿ, Yūnus and Lūt; We preferred them all over the entire creation. And [We guided] certain [individuals from] their ancestors, their descendants and their brothers; We chose them and We guided them to a straight path. That is Allāh's guidance by which He guides whoever He wills of His servants. However if they had associated others with Allāh [in His divinity] then whatever [good] they were doing would become worthless for them. Those are the ones whom We gave the scripture, authority and prophet hood to. [. . .] Those are the ones who Allāh guided; so follow their guidance." (Sūrat al-Anʿām 6:84–90)

"And We sent every messenger simply to be obeyed by Allāh's permission." (Sūrat al-Nisāʾ 4:64)

51 "And our messengers had certainly come to them with clear proofs." (Sūrat al-Māʾidah 5:32)

"And a messenger could not come with a sign except through Allāh's permission." (Sūrat al-Raʿd 13:38)

52 "These messengers; We have given superiority to some of them over others [among them]. There were those among them who Allāh spoke [directly] to, and He raised some of them in ranks. And We gave clear proofs to ʿĪsā, the son of Maryam, and We supported him with the Pure Spirit." (Sūrat al-Baqarah 2:253)

"And Allāh took Ibrāhīm as a dear friend." (Sūrat al-Nisāʾ 4:125)

53 "And We have already sent messengers before you. Among them are those whose stories We have related to you, and among them are those whose stories We have not related to you." (Sūrat al-Ghāfir 40:78)

- The Prophet Muḥammad ﷺ is Allāh's final messenger to humanity.[54]
- The Prophet Muḥammad ﷺ was a mercy for every creation. What bothered others bothered him.[55]
- The Prophet Muḥammad ﷺ was appointed by Allāh ﷻ to:
  - (1) Convey Allāh's message to humanity.
  - (2) Educate people about Allāh ﷻ and the way of life that pleases Allāh ﷻ.
  - (3) Steer people away from misguidance and direct them to the straight path.[56]

---

54 "Muḥammad is not the father of any one of your men, however he is Allāh's Messenger of and the seal of the prophets." (Sūrat al-Aḥzāb 33:40)

Jābir ؓ reported, "The Prophet ﷺ said, '[. . .] I have come and concluded the [chain of] Prophets.'" (*Ṣaḥīḥ Muslim* 5963)

Anas ibn Mālik ؓ reported, "Allāh's Messenger ﷺ said, 'Indeed the message [of the Divine] and prophethood has come to an end; hence there will be no messenger or prophet after me." (*Jāmiʿ al-Tirmidhī* 2272)

55 "A messenger has certainly come to you from among you. What you suffer puts him in grief. He is concerned about you, and is kind and merciful to the believers." (Sūrat al-Tawbah 10:128)

"And We have sent you, Muḥammad, simply as a mercy for every creation." (Sūrat al-Anbiyāʾ 21:107)

56 "Prophet, indeed We have sent you as a witness, a bringer of good news and as a warner. And as one who invites to Allāh, by His permission, and as an illuminating lamp." (Sūrat al-Aḥzāb 33:45–46)

"Messenger, pass along [to others] everything that has been revealed to you from your Master. And if you do not [do as such] then you have not conveyed His message." (Sūrat al-Māʾidah 5:67)

"[. . .] We have sent a messenger among you who is from you. He recites Our verses to you, purifies you, teaches you the Book and wisdom. And he teaches you things which you did not know." (Sūrat al-Baqarah 2:151)

- The Prophet Muḥammad ﷺ was neither divine nor did he possess absolute knowledge of unseen realities (*ghayb*).[57]

WHAT ARE MY BELIEFS IN THE DIVINE DECREE AND DESTINY (*QADR*)?

- Allāh ﷻ produced us along with the entire creation and established our fate and destiny.[58]
- Our actions were never concealed from Allāh ﷻ before He created us. He knew what we were going to do before bringing us into existence.[59]
- Favourable and unfavourable conditions are decreed for each and every one of us.[60]
- The options of our actions are created by Allāh ﷻ and then selected and carried out by us. Once we do an action the action is considered to be our own acquisition.[61]

---

57 "Say, 'Exalted is my Master! I am only a messenger [of Allāh who is] human.'" (Sūrat al-Isrāʾ 17:93)

"Say, 'I cannot control benefit or harm for myself, except what Allāh has willed. And if I knew the unseen [realities], I would have amassed a great amount of wealth. And no harm would have [ever] come in contact with me. I am only a warner and a bringer of good news to a community who believes.'" (Sūrat al-Aʿrāf 7:188)

58 "Indeed, We created all things with predestination." (Sūrat al-Qamar 54:49)

59 "And no soul knows what it will earn tomorrow, and no soul knows what land it will die in. Indeed, Allāh is Knowing and Ever-Acquainted." (Sūrat Luqmān 31:34)

60 "But if good comes to them, they say, 'This is from Allāh,' and if evil befalls them, they say, 'This is from you.' Say, 'Everything is from Allāh.'" (Sūrat al-Nisāʾ 4:78)

61 "Allāh created you and everything you do." (Sūrat al-Ṣāffāt 37:96)

"Allāh only compels a soul to [do] what is in its capacity. The soul will receive the

- Everything occurs according to Allāh's will. His will is fulfilled in every circumstance.[62] We can only will what Allāh ﷻ allows us to will.
- Allāh ﷻ guides whomever He wills out of His grace and leaves astray whomever He wills out of justice.[63]
- We believe in the Tablet and the Pen along with everything that was inscribed in the Tablet.[64]
- Every situation a person is spared from could not have afflicted him, and everything that afflicts him could not have missed him.[65]

---

results of the good it earned, and will face [the consequences of] the [evil] it earned." (Sūrat al-Baqarah 2:286)

"Then every soul will be fully compensated for what it earned, and they will not be wronged." (Sūrat Āle ʿImrān 3:161)

62 "Indeed, Allāh does what He wills." (Sūrat al-Ḥajj 22:18)

"And you will only wish what Allāh wills. Indeed, Allāh is ever Knowing and Wise." (Sūrat al-Insān 76:30)

"But if your Master had willed, they would not have done it. So leave them [alone] and whatever they make up." (Sūrat al-Anʿām 6:112)

63 "And Allāh guides who He likes to [the] straight path." (Sūrat al-Baqarah 2:213)

"Allāh selects who He likes for His mercy, and Allāh possesses the great bounty." (Sūrat al-Baqarah 2:105)

"Indeed, Allāh leaves astray who He wills and guides to Himself whoever turns back to Him." (Sūrat al-Raʿd 13:27)

"And Allāh leaves the wrongdoers astray. And Allāh does as He pleases." (Sūrat Ibrāhīm 14:27)

64 "But this is an honourable Qur'ān [that is] inscribed in a protected Tablet." (Sūrat al-Burūj 85:21–22)

"Nūn. [I swear] by the pen and what [the angels] inscribe." (Sūrat al-Qalam 68:1)

65 "Say, 'We will only be afflicted with what Allāh has decreed for us.'" (Sūrat al-Tawbah 9:51)

"No disaster strikes upon the earth or among yourselves except that it is [already documented] in a register before We bring it into existence. Indeed that is easy for Allāh. [Allāh is informing you of this] so that you do not become distressed over what

- The essence of the divine decree is Allāh's secret. No angel or prophet has knowledge of it. Investigating it and reflecting over it will cause you to become extremely confused. Ultimately it will lead you astray. So abstain from pondering over it and accepting satanic whispers about it.[66]

WHAT ARE MY BELIEFS IN THE FINAL DAY?

- The Day of Resurrection is a day that is real and true.[67]
- It will occur after the final day of this world. The appointed angel will blow the horn on the final day due to which all life will come to an end.[68] After that the entire solar system will be completely destroyed.[69]

---

has missed you and you do not take pride in what He has given you. And Allāh does not like every conceited and boastful person." (Sūrat al-Ḥadīd 57:22–23)

66 "And the keys of the Unseen are with Him; no one knows them except Him. And He knows what is on the land and in the sea. Neither a leaf falls but He knows of it nor is there a grain within the darknesses of the earth, nor is there something moist or dry except that it is [all] written in a clear record." (Sūrat al-Anʿām 6:59)

67 "He will definitely bring you all together for the Day of Resurrection, about which there is no doubt." (Sūrat al-Anʿām 6:12)

68 "And the Horn will be blown. Everyone in the heavens and the earth will fall dead except who Allāh wishes [to spare]." (Sūrat al-Zumar 39:68)

"Everyone on Earth will perish. [However] the Face of your Master who is the Possessor of Majesty and Honour will remain." (Sūrat al-Raḥmān 55:26–27)

69 "When the sun will be wrapped up in darkness and when the stars will fall dispersing, and when the mountains will be removed and when full-term she-camels will be neglected and when wild beasts will be gathered and when the seas will be filled with flame." (Sūrat al-Takwīr 81:1–6)

"When the sky breaks apart and when the stars fall scattering and when the seas erupt and when the contents of the graves become scattered." (Sūrat al-Infiṭār 82:1–4)

"When Earth will be shaken with its final earthquake, and it will emit its burdens, and people will say, 'What is wrong with [Earth]?'" (Sūrat al-Zalzalah 99:1–3)

- Upon the second sounding of the horn, the dead will rise from their graves.[70]
- Everybody will be gathered at one location in front of Allāh ﷻ.[71] No one will be able to hide or escape.[72]
- On that day Allāh ﷻ Himself will come forth to assess His creation's compliance to His orders in this world. After the assessment He will make His final evaluation.[73]
- The believers will be able to see Allāh ﷻ while the disbelievers will be deprived of witnessing His magnificence.[74]
- *Jannah* and *Jahannam* will be brought forth.[75]

---

70 "Then it will be blown again, and at once they will be standing, looking on." (Sūrat al-Zumar 39:68)

"And the Horn will be blown; and at once [people] will rush from [their] graves to their Sustainer. They will say, 'Woe to us! Who has raised us up from our sleeping place?' [They will be told], 'This is what the Most Merciful had promised, and the messengers told the truth.'" (Sūrat Yāsīn 36:52–53)

71 "[On] that day you will be presented [for judgement]; nothing that is hidden among you is going to be concealed." (Sūrat al-Ḥāqqah 69:18)

72 "And be mindful of Allāh and know that you will be gathered in front of Him." (Sūrat al-Baqarah 2:203)

"And all creatures will come out before Allāh, the One, the Prevailing." (Sūrat Ibrāhīm 14:48)

73 "And your Master has come [along with] the angels, rank upon rank." (Sūrat al-Fajr 89:22)

"And above them that day, eight angels will carry the throne of your Master." (Sūrat al-Ḥāqqah 69:17)

74 "[On] that day some faces will be radiant. They will be looking at their Master." (Sūrat al-Qiyāmah 75:22–23)

"No! Indeed, they will be screened off from their Master that Day." (Sūrat al-Muṭaffifīn 83:15)

75 "And [on] that day Jannah will be brought close to the righteous. And Hellfire will be brought before those who deviated [from the straight path]." (Sūrat al-Shuʿrāʾ 26:90–91)

- The Scale will be presented and people's deeds will be weighed on it.[76]
- Those whose good deeds outweigh their evil deeds will be given their life journal(s) in their right hand and will be admitted into *Jannah*.[77]
- As for those whose bad deeds outweigh their good deeds, they will be either be sent to the Fire of *Jahannam* or pardoned by Allāh ﷻ.
- Allāh ﷻ will be prepared to forgive everything on that day except for polytheism (*shirk*) and disbelief (*kufr*).[78]

---

76 "And We will put the scales of justice [in their place] for the Day of Rising. No soul will be treated unjustly at all. And even if there is [a deed] the weight of a mustard seed, We will bring it forth. And We are sufficient to [independently] take [everyone's] accounts." (Sūrat al-Anbiyā' 21:47)

"So whoever does an atom's weight of good will see it. And whoever does an atom's weight of evil will see it." (Sūrat al-Zalzalah 99:7–8)

77 "Then as for one whose scales are heavy with good deeds, he will [have] a pleasant life." (Sūrat al-Qāriʿah 101:6–7)

"So as for the one, who is given his record in his right hand, he will say, 'Here, read my record! Indeed, I was certain that I would be meeting my account.' So he will be in a pleasant life in an elevated garden, its fruit will be hanging near to be picked. They will be told, 'Eat and drink in satisfaction due to what you put forth in the past days.'" (Sūrat al-Ḥāqqah 69:19–24)

78 "But as for the one whose scales are light, his shelter will be an abyss. And what can make you know what that [really] is? It is an intensely hot fire." (Sūrat al-Qāriʿah 101:8–11)

"But as for the one who is given his record in his left hand, he will say, 'Oh I wish I had not been given my record. I had not known what my account is. I wish my death had been decisive. My wealth has not benefitted me. My authority is gone from me.' Allāh will say, 'Seize him and shackle him, and then drive him into the Hellfire. After that, place him into a chain whose length is seventy cubits [32 metres].'" (Sūrat al-Ḥāqqah 69: 25–32)

"Indeed, Allāh will not forgive any association with Him [in His divinity], but He will forgive whom He wills for [any sin that] is less than that. And he who associates others with Allāh has certainly gone far astray." (Sūrat al-Nisā' 4:116)

"And thus the word of your Master has come into effect upon those who disbelieved, that they are the people of the Fire." (Sūrat al-Ghāfir 40:6)

Legal (*Fiqh*) Terms

LEGAL (*FIQH*) TERMINOLOGY

Farḍ

Farḍ[79] is a command that is taken directly from either the Qur'ān, the *Mutawātir Aḥādīth*[80] or the consensus (*ijmāʿ*) of the Prophet's companions (*ṣaḥābah*).[81] You are obligated to believe in it and practice it. You will become a disbeliever (*kāfir*) by rejecting it, and a sinner (*fāsiq*) for neglecting it.

Farḍ is divided into two categories:

1. *Farḍ al-ʿAyn*: a duty you must execute provided you are qualified. You will be relieved of the duty only after performing it, e.g. five daily ritual prayers (*ṣalāh*), fasting (*ṣawm*), and wealth purification (*zakāh*).
2. *Farḍ al-Kifāyah*: a duty which an unspecified number of people from the community must carry out. By them carrying this duty out, the remainder of the community will be relieved of it, e.g. bathing the deceased and participating in the funeral prayer.

---

79 The following has been adapted from *Kawāshif al-Jalīyah ʿan Muṣṭalaḥāt al-Ḥanafīyah* by ʿAbd al-Ilāh ibn Muḥammad al-Mullā.

80 *Mutawātir Aḥādīth* are *ḥadīths* that;

- Have been reported by so many people that it impossible for them to have planned to make up the account or. . .
- . . .to coincidently have reported the same false account collectively.
- Have a consistent number of reporters from the beginning of their transmission chain (*isnād*) to their end.
- Are eye-witnessed accounts by the original reporters.
- Convince people that the incident really happened.

81 *Nūr al-Anwār* p.222

Wājib

Wājib is an order that is taken from the *Akhbār al-Āḥād*.[82] You must practise it, however you will not be considered a disbeliever for rejecting it. Examples of *wājib* duties are *ṣadaqat al-fiṭr* and offering a sacrifice during *ʿĪd al-Aḍ'ḥā*.

Sunnah

Sunnah is a practice of our beloved Prophet Muḥammad ﷺ. It is an activity that is neither *farḍ* nor *wājib*.

Sunnah is divided into two categories:

1. *Sunnat al-Mu'akkadah*: a practice that should not be neglected, such as the calls to prayer (*adhān* and *iqāmah*) and participating in congregational prayers.
2. *Sunnat Ghayr al-Mu'akkadah*: a practice that will not have any negative spiritual consequence if neglected.

Mustaḥabb

Mustaḥabb is a religious activity that is neither *farḍ*, *wājib* nor *sunnah*. You will be rewarded by Allāh ﷻ for practising it and you will not face any negative repercussions for neglecting it.

Mustaḥabb is also called *Adab*, *Mandūb*, *Nafl* and *Taṭawwūʿ*.

Mubāḥ

Mubāḥ is an activity which you will neither be rewarded for doing nor punished for forsaking.

---

82 *Akhbār al-Āḥād* are *ḥadīths* whose reporters are not as numerous as *Mutawātir Aḥādīth*.

Makrūh

Makrūh is an action you should avoid. *Makrūh* is divided into two categories:

1. *Makrūh Tanzīh*: an action you will be rewarded by Allāh ﷻ for avoiding. However, if you do it, you will not face any adverse repercussions.
2. *Makrūh Taḥrīm*: a prohibition that is taken from the *Akhbār al-Āḥād*. You must refrain from committing such actions however you will not be termed a disbeliever for rejecting it.

Examples of actions that are *Makrūh Taḥrīm* are:

- Men wearing gold jewellery
- Men wearing silk clothing

Normally when jurists use the term *makrūh* in general, they refer to *taḥrīm*.

Ḥarām

Ḥarām is a prohibition that is taken directly from either the Qur'ān, the *Mutawātir Aḥādīth* or the *ijmā*ʿ of *Ṣaḥābah*. You are required to believe in the prohibition. By rejecting it you will become a *kāfir* and by doing it you will become a *fāsiq*.

Purification
(*Ṭahārah*)

WHY IS PURITY IMPORTANT IN ISLAM?

Our beloved Prophet ﷺ once explained, "Purity is half of faith (*īmān*)."[83] If you try your best to remain pure at all times, Allāh ﷻ will love you; "*Allāh loves those who purify themselves.*"[84]

Bathing (Ghusl)

WHEN AM I REQUIRED TO TAKE A FULL RITUAL SHOWER OR BATH (*GHUSL*)?

You must bathe when you are in the state of major ritual impurity (*janābah*).[85] If you are a woman, you must bathe at the end of your menses (*ḥayḍ*) or at the end of your postnatal bleeding (*nifās*).[86]

Janābah is constituted when;

- The glans penetrates beyond the labia when having sexual intercourse.[87]
- You have a wet dream.[88]

---

83 *Ṣaḥīḥ Muslim* 534

84 Sūrat al-Tawbah 9:108

85 "You who have believed, do not approach ritual prayer while intoxicated until you know what you are saying, or when ritually impure (janābah), except those passing through [a place of prayer], until you have washed [your whole body] [. . .]."(Sūrat al-Nisā' 4:43)

"[. . .] and if you are ritually impure, then purify yourselves [. . .]." (Sūrat al-Mā'idah 5:6)

86 "And they ask you about menstruation. Say, 'It is harmful, so keep away from [having sex with your] wives during [their] menses. And do not approach them [for sex] until they become pure [. . .]." (Sūrat al-Baqarah 2:222)

87 'Ā'ishah ؓ reported, "Allāh's Messenger ﷺ said, 'When the glans penetrates beyond the labia, a complete *ghusl* becomes compulsory.'" (*Jāmiʿ al-Tirmidhī* 109)

88 Umm Salamah ؓ reported, "Umm Sulaym, Abū Ṭalha's wife ؓ, came to

◇ A man ejaculates after engaging in some other form of sexual activity e.g. masturbation, viewing sexual material (both of which are prohibited in Islam).

WHAT ARE THE *FARḌ* ACTS OF *GHUSL*?

There are three *farḍ* activities in *ghusl*:

1. To gargle the mouth.[89]

2. To clean out the nose with water.

3. To wash the entire body in a manner that not a single hair is left dry.[90]

It is important that:

◇ All areas of the body are washed thoroughly with water. The inner part of the penile foreskin and the labia majora must also be washed.

◇ The inner part of the navel is washed.

◇ You untie your braids if you are a man, even if water reaches your scalp.

Allāh's Messenger ﷺ and asked, 'Messenger of Allāh, Allāh is not ashamed of the truth; is a woman required to bathe if she has a wet dream?'

Allāh's Messenger ﷺ replied, 'Yes, when she sees discharge.'" (*Ṣaḥīḥ al-Bukhārī* 282)

89 'Ā'ishah bint 'Ajrad said about a person in the state of *janābah* who forgets to cleanse their mouth and nose, "Ibn 'Abbās ◈ said, '[That person] will [have to] rinse out their mouth and nose and repeat [their] *ṣalāh*." (*Sunan al-Dārquṭnī* 408)

90 'Alī ◈ stated, "Whoever leaves out the area of a hair's span (when bathing) from *janābah*, and does not wash it; something will be done to him in the Fire [of Hell]." (*Sunan Abū Dāwūd* 249)

◇ If you are a woman, you are exempt from undoing your braids as long as water reaches your scalp.[91] However if your hair is so compact that it prevents water from penetrating your hair, you must also undo your braids.

◇ Water reaches the skin beneath your beard, moustache and eyebrows.

WHAT IS THE SUNNAH METHOD OF PERFORMING GHUSL?

◇ Wash both hands.[92]

◇ Wash your private parts with your left hand.

◇ Wash away all impure bodily fluids found on your body. After that wash your hands.

---

91 Umm Salamah ⁕ said, "I [once] asked, 'Messenger of Allāh, I am a woman who [ties] braids in my head. Will I [have to] untie them when bathing from *janābah?*' The Prophet ⁕ said, 'No. Throwing water over your head three times is sufficient for you. After that, you are to pour water over your [entire body] and thus obtain the state of purity.'" (*Ṣaḥīḥ Muslim* 744)

92 Maymūnah ⁕ said, "I poured water [into a container] for the Prophet ⁕ for [his] bath. [When he went for his bath] he poured water onto his left hand with his right hand and washed them both. Then he washed his private parts and then rubbed his hand on the ground and washed it. He then rinsed his mouth and cleaned his nose out with water. After that, he washed his face and poured water on his head. Then he moved to one side and washed his feet. He was then given a towel [to dry himself with] but did not use it." (*Ṣaḥīḥ al-Bukhārī* 259)

'Ā'ishah ⁕ related, "Whenever the Prophet ⁕ took a bath to exit the state of *janābah*, he would begin by washing his hands and would then perform *wuḍū'* as he would for *ṣalāh*. After that, he would put his fingers in the water and massage the roots of his hair with them. After that he would pour three handfuls [of water] on his head and would then pour water over his entire body." (*Ṣaḥīḥ al-Bukhārī* 248)

◇ Perform your ablutions (*wuḍū'*).

◇ Pour water on your head three times.

◇ Wash the entire body three times.

◇ Wash your feet separately after leaving the bathtub or shower room if the water is slow to drain.

Ritual Ablution (*Wuḍū'*)

WHY IS RITUAL ABLUTION (*WUḌŪ'*) IMPORTANT?

Wuḍū' is a prerequisite for ritual prayer (*ṣalāh*).[93] Without it, Allāh ﷻ will not accept your *ṣalāh*.[94]

WHAT ARE THE *FARḌ* ACTS OF *WUḌŪ'*?

There are four *farḍ* activities in *wuḍū'*:

1. To wash the entire face. Technically the face is vertically from the point where the hairline normally begins to the bottom of the chin, and horizontally from earlobe to earlobe.

2. To wash the arms up to and including the elbows.

3. To wipe a quarter of the head with a moist hand.

---

93 "You who believe, when you rise for *ṣalāh*, wash your faces and your hands up to the elbows, and wipe [a portion] of your heads [with a wet hand] and [wash] your feet up to the ankles." (*Sūrat al-Mā'idah* 5:6)

94 Ibn 'Umar ﵁ reported, The Prophet ﷺ said, 'No *ṣalāh* is accepted without [ritual] purification.'" (*Jāmiʿ al-Tirmidhī* 1)

4. To wash the feet up to and including the ankles.[95]

WHAT IS THE SUNNAH METHOD OF PERFORMING *WUḌŪ'*?

- Brush your teeth with a natural tooth stick (*miswāk*).[96]
- Make the intention to perform *wuḍū'* for the sake of exiting the state of minor ritual impurity (*ḥadath al-asghar*) to worship Allāh ﷻ and please Him.[97]
- Say *bismillāh*.[98]
- Wash both hands up to and including the wrists.[99]

---

95 See footnote 93

96 'Ā'ishah ؓ reported, "Whenever the Prophet ﷺ went to sleep during the night or day and then woke up, he would brush his teeth before performing *wuḍū'*." (*Sunan Abū Dāwūd* 57)

97 'Umar ibn al-Khaṭṭāb ؓ narrated, "I heard Allāh's Messenger ﷺ say, 'Deeds are solely dependent on intentions, and every person will receive what they intended [. . .].'" (*Ṣaḥīḥ al-Bukhārī* 1)

98 Allāh's Messenger ﷺ said, "There is no *wuḍū'* for a person who does not mention Allāh's name [before performing] it." (*Jāmi' al-Tirmidhī* 25)

99 'Amr ؓ reported from his father who related, "I saw 'Amr ibn Abū Ḥasan ؓ ask 'Abdullāh ibn Zayd ؓ about the Prophet's ﷺ *wuḍū'*. For this purpose, 'Abdullāh asked for a pot of water and then demonstrated the *wuḍū'* of the Prophet ﷺ to them. He poured the pot [of water] over his hand and washed his hands three times. He then put his hand into the pot, [drew water from it] and rinsed his mouth. He sniffed the water with three handfuls to clean out his nose. After that, he put his hand into the pot [to get more water] and washed his face three times. He then washed both of his arms up to his elbows twice. Then he dipped his hand into the pot and wiped his head by passing both hands from the front to the back and [then] from the back to the front once. He then [concluded by] washing both his feet up to his ankles." (*Ṣaḥīḥ al-Bukhārī* 186)

- Using water, rinse your mouth out three times with your right hand.[100] Use fresh water for each rinse.[101]

- Clean your nose out thoroughly three times provided you are not fasting.[102] Insert fresh water in your nose each time with your right hand and then clean it out with your left hand.[103]

- Wash your face three times.[104] Avoid any delay between the washes.

- Wash your right forearm three times up to and including your elbow. Begin the wash from your fingers and work your way to your elbow. Then wash your left forearm in the same manner.[105]

- If you have a ring on, slide it away from its place to wash the covered area.[106]

---

100 Abū Ḥayyah reported, "I saw ʿAlī ﷺ perform *wuḍūʾ*. He washed both of his hands until they were clean. Then he rinsed his mouth three times and cleaned out his nose with water three times. He washed his face three times and his arms three times. He then wiped his head once and washed his feet up to the ankles. After that he stood and took the remainder of his [clean] water and drank it while standing. He then said, "I wanted to show you what the ablutions of Allāh's Messenger ﷺ was like." (*Jāmiʿ al-Tirmidhī* 48)

101 See footnote 99

102 Laqīṭ ibn Ṣabirah ﷺ reported, "[. . .] I asked, 'Messenger of Allāh, tell me about *wuḍūʾ*.' The Messenger ﷺ replied, 'Perform *wuḍūʾ* properly. Clean [your] nose out thoroughly except when you're fasting.'" (*Sunan Abū Dāwūd* 142)

103 ʿĀʾishah ﷺ related, "The right hand of Allāh's Messenger ﷺ was used for attaining purity and for eating, whereas his left hand was used for the washroom and unclean affairs." (*Sunan Abū Dāwūd* 33)

104 See footnote 99

105 ʿĀʾishah ﷺ reported, "The Prophet ﷺ liked beginning with the right as much as possible in all his affairs; when attaining ritual purity, combing his hair and putting on his shoes." (*Ṣaḥīḥ al-Bukhārī* 426)

106 Abū Rāfiʿ ﷺ reported, "Allāh's Messenger ﷺ would move his ring when

- Place your left hand above your right hand, palms facing down. Slide the fingers of the left hand between the fingers of the right hand. Then repeat this action with your right hand on top.[107]

- Wipe your head once by running both hands while they are moist along it. Begin from the normal hairline and draw your hands from the front to the back, then from the back to the front.[108]

- Clean your ears with your moist hands without wetting them again. Use your index fingers to clean the inside portion of your ears and the thumbs to clean behind your ears.[109]

- Wash the right foot three times. Begin each wash by cleaning between your toes with the baby finger of your left hand and then gradually move towards your ankles. Then wash the left foot in the same manner.[110]

- Stand up and drink some water.[111]

---

performing *wuḍū'*." (*Sunan Ibn Mājah* 449)

107 Laqīṭ ibn Ṣabirah reported, "The Prophet said, 'When you perform *wuḍū'*, pass the fingers [of one hand between the fingers of the other]." (*Jāmiʿ al-Tirmidhī* 38)

108 See footnote 99

109 Ibn 'Abbās reported, "Allāh's Messenger performed *wuḍū'*. He took a handful of water and rinsed his mouth and cleaned out his nose. He then took another handful of water and washed his face. After that, he took another handful of water and washed his right arm. He then took another handful of water and washed his left arm. He then wiped his head and ears; the internal portion [of his ear] with [his] index finger and the external portion with his thumb. Then he took a handful of water and washed his right foot and then took a handful of water and washed his left foot. (*Sunan al-Nasa'ī* 102)

110 See footnote 100

111 ibid.

◇ Recite:

$$\text{أَشْهَدُ أَنْ لَا إِلٰهَ إِلَّا اللّٰهُ وَحْدَهُ لَا شَرِيْكَ لَهُ وَ}$$

$$\text{أَشْهَدُ أَنَّ مُحَمَّدًا عَبْدُهُ وَرَسُوْلُهُ. اَللّٰهُمَّ اجْعَلْنِيْ}$$

$$\text{مِنَ التَّوَّابِيْنَ واجْعَلْنِيْ مِنَ الْمُتَطَهِّرِيْنَ.}$$

*Ash'hadu allā ilāha illallāhu waḥdahū lā sharīka
lahū wa-ash'hadu anna Muḥammadan 'ab-
duhū wa-rasūluh. Allāhumma j'alnī min at-taw-
wābīna wa-j'alnī mina l-mutaṭahhirīn.*

I testify that there is no god but Allāh, who
is One and without any partner. I testify that
Muḥammad is Allāh's servant and messenger. O
Allāh, make me of those who repent often and
make me of those who keep themselves pure.[112]

---

112 'Umar ibn al-Khaṭṭāb ☙ reported, "Allāh's Messenger ﷺ said, 'Whoever performs *wuḍū*, does it well, and then recites, 'I testify that there is no god but Allāh, who is One and without any partner. I testify that Muḥammad is Allāh's servant and messenger. O Allāh, make me of those who repent often. Make me of those who keep themselves pure,' the eight gates of Paradise will be opened for that person. They may enter from whichever gate they please.'" (*Jāmi' al-Tirmidhī* 55)

WHAT NULLIFIES *WUḌŪ'*?

- Anything that comes out of the urinary, vaginal and anal passages.[113]
- The flowing of impure matter from anywhere else on the body such as blood, pus etc.[114]
- To throw up in a manner that the vomit cannot be contained in the mouth.[115]
- To sleep while lying down on your back or reclining on your side.[116]
- Losing consciousness.
- Losing sanity.
- Laughing aloud during *ṣalāh*, except during the funeral prayer.[117]

---

113 "You who believe, when you rise to [perform] ṣalāh, wash your face and your forearms to the elbows and wipe over your head and wash your feet to the ankles. And if you are in a state of janābah, then purify yourselves. But if you are ill or on a journey or one of you comes from the place of relieving himself or you have had intimate relations with women, and cannot find water, then seek clean earth and wipe it over your face and hands [. . .]." (Sūrat al-Mā'idah 5:6)

Abū Hurayrah ﷺ reported, "Allāh's Messenger ﷺ said, 'The *ṣalāh* of one who enters the state of *ḥadath* is not accepted until they perform *wuḍū'*.'" A man from Ḥaḍramawt asked, 'What is *ḥadath*, Abū Hurayrah?' He said, '[Passing] gas.'" (*Ṣaḥīḥ al-Bukhārī* 135)

114 'Ā'ishah ﷺ narrated that the Prophet ﷺ said, "Whoever vomits, has a nosebleed, a reflux or some pre-seminal discharge [while performing *ṣalāh*], should turn away [from *ṣalāh* i.e. discontinue it] and perform *wuḍū'*." (*Sunan Ibn Mājah* 1221)

115 ibid.

116 'Alī ibn Abū Ṭālib ﷺ reported, "Allāh's Messenger ﷺ said, 'The eyes are the draw-strings of the anus. So whoever goes to sleep should perform *wuḍū'*.'" (*Sunan Abū Dāwūd* 203)

117 Abū Mūsā ﷺ said, "[Once] while the Prophet ﷺ led people in *ṣalāh* a man

Fiqh Principle: Certainty is not removed by doubt. Never discontinue your *ṣalāh* until you are absolutely sure that your *wuḍū'* is nullified.[118]

entered [the Masjid] and fell into a well that was in the Masjid. He had poor eyesight. Many people laughed while they were engaged in *ṣalāh*. [Upon concluding the prayer] Allāh's Messenger ﷺ instructed those who laughed to redo their *wuḍū'* and to repeat their *ṣalāh*." (*Majma' al-Zawā'id* 1278)

118 A complaint was received by the Prophet ﷺ about a man who assumed he experienced something [that nullifies *wuḍū'* while performing] *ṣalāh*. The Prophet ﷺ explained, "He should not turn away (i.e. discontinue his *ṣalāh*) until he hears a sound or senses a [foul] odour." (*Ṣaḥīḥ Muslim* 804)

Ritual Prayer
(*Ṣalāh*)

WHY IS RITUAL PRAYER (*ṢALĀH*) IMPORTANT?

Ṣalāh is one of the integral practices of Islam. Allāh ﷻ has ordered that we perform it regularly and punctually to remember Him;

- "[. . .] establish prayer for My remembrance."[119]
- "Maintain the [obligatory] prayers with care [. . .]."[120]

By exercising this command with concentration and care, you will become continuously conscious of Allāh ﷻ. This awareness is what will save you from Allāh's disobedience thus earning you the best of accommodations in the hereafter;

- "Indeed, ritual prayer prevents [you from] immorality and wrongdoing [. . .]."[121]
- "And they who carefully maintain their ritual prayers, those are the inheritors who will inherit Firdous.[122] They will eternally abide therein."[123]

WHAT ARE THE PRECONDITIONS OF *ṢALĀH*?

- To become ritually pure from major and minor ritual impurities (*ḥadath al-akbar* & *ḥadath al-asghar*).[124]

---

119 Sūrat Ṭāhā 20:14

120 Sūrat al-Baqarah 2:238

121 Sūrat al-ʿAnkabūt 29:45

122 The highest level of Paradise

123 Sūrat al-Muʾminūn 23:9–11

124 "You who believe, when you rise to [perform] ṣalāh, wash your face and your forearms to the elbows, wipe your head and wash your feet to the ankles. And if you are in a state of janābah, then purify yourselves." (Sūrat al-Māʾidah 5:6)

- Your body and clothes must be free from impure substances.[125]
- Your private areas (*ʿawrah*) must be covered.[126]
- The place where you will perform *ṣalāh* must be clean.[127]
- You must ensure that the time of *ṣalāh* has begun.[128]
- You must face the ritual prayer direction (*qiblah*).[129]
- You must make an intention to perform a particular *ṣalāh* prior to beginning that *ṣalāh*.[130]
- You must perform your previously missed ritual prayers before performing the current *ṣalāh*, provided that the

---

125 "And purify your clothing." (Sūrat al-Muddath'thir 74:4)
Examples of impure substances are:

- Urine
- Faecal matter
- Seminal fluid
- Blood
- Wine
- The saliva of dogs, pigs and predatory animals

126 "Children of Ādam, take your adornment to every Masjid" (Sūrat al-Aʿrāf 7:31)

- The *ʿawrah* of a man is from the navel to just below the knees.
- The *ʿawrah* of a woman is her entire body excluding her face and hands up to the wrists.

127 "And We instructed Ibrāhīm and Ismāʿīl, saying, 'Purify My House for those who will perform ṭawāf, and for those who will stay there for worship, and for those who will bow and prostrate in prayer." (Sūrat al-Baqarah 2:125)

128 "Indeed, ṣalāh has been decreed upon the believers with specified times." (Sūrat al-Nisāʾ 4:103)

129 "So turn your face toward Masjid al-Ḥarām. And wherever you may be, turn your faces toward it [in ṣalāh]." (Sūrat al-Baqarah 2:144)

130 "And they were simply instructed to worship Allāh, being sincere to Him [. . .]" (Sūrat al-Bayyinah 98:5)

number of your missed ritual prayers is less than five and there is enough time for you to perform them all before the time of the current *ṣalāh* runs out.[131]

- You must avoid standing ahead of the imam in a congregational prayer. A congregant must stand behind the imam at all times.[132]

WHAT ARE THE INTEGRAL PRACTICES OF *ṢALĀH*?

- If you are able, you must stand during the obligatory (*farḍ*) prayer.[133]
- You must begin *ṣalāh* with the opening *takbīr* (*takbīrat al-taḥrīm*).[134]
- You must recite at least three short verses or one lengthy verse of the Qur'ān.[135]
- You must bow (*rukūʿ*).[136]

---

131 Anas ibn Mālik ﷺ reported, "The Prophet of Allāh ﷺ said, 'Whoever forgets to [perform] *ṣalāh* or sleeps through [an entire period of *ṣalāh*], its amendment is to perform it when [you] remember it.'" (*Ṣaḥīḥ Muslim* 1568)

132 Anas ibn Mālik ﷺ reported that his grandmother invited Allāh's Messenger ﷺ for some food, which she prepared. He partook of the meal and then said, 'Stand so I can lead you in *ṣalāh*.' [. . .] So I stood [and went to get a] straw mat of ours that had become black due to the length it had been around. I sprinkled it with some water and then Allāh's Messenger ﷺ stood on it. I formed a row behind him with the orphan while the elderly woman [stood] behind us. Allāh's Messenger ﷺ then performed two *rakaʿāt* for us and left thereafter." (*Ṣaḥīḥ Muslim* 1499)

133 "[. . .] and stand before Allāh, devoutly obedient." (Sūrat al-Baqarah 2:238)

134 "And glorify your Sustainer." (Sūrat al-Muddath'thir 74:3)

135 "[. . .] so recite what is easy [for you] of the Qur'ān [. . .]." (Sūrat al-Muzzammil 73:20)

136 "You who believe, bow and prostrate and worship your Master [. . .]."

⬦ You must prostrate (*sujūd*).[137]

⬦ You must perform the final sitting for the duration of reciting the *tashahhud*.[138]

WHAT ARE THE *WĀJIB* ACTIONS OF *ṢALĀH*?

Before ṣalāh:

⬦ You must perform *ṣalāh* in congregation if you are a male and reside near a masjid.[139] If you're a female you may also visit the masjid[140] however it is preferable for you to perform your *ṣalāh* at home.[141]

(Sūrat al-Ḥajj 22:77)

137 ibid.

138 'Abdullāh ibn Masʿūd ⬦ reported that Allāh's Messenger ⬦ took hold of his hand and taught him the *tashahhud* (which is to be recited) during *ṣalāh*. [. . .] [He then said,] "When you say this—or—complete this, then you have completed your *ṣalāh*. If you would like to stand [to go on your way], you may stand and if you would like to remain seated, you may remain seated." (*Sunan Abū Dāwūd* 970)

139 "[. . .] and bow with those who bow [in worship]." (Sūrat al-Baqarah 2:43) Abū Hurayrah ⬦ reported, "Allāh's Messenger ⬦ said, 'I intended to instruct [some people] to collect some firewood. Then I [wanted to] give the order for *ṣalāh*, subsequently the *adhān* would have been given. Then I [wanted to] instruct a person to lead people in prayer. Then I [wanted to] remain absent from the prayer and pursue those men [who fail to attend it] and burn their houses down on them. [. . .]'" (*Ṣaḥīḥ al-Bukhārī* 644)

140 Abū Hurayrah ⬦ reported, "Allāh's Messenger ⬦ said, 'Do not prevent the female servants of Allāh (i.e. women) from [going to] the *masājid* of Allāh. However they should go out [looking] unattractive.'" (*Sunan Abū Dāwūd* 565)

141 Umm Salamah ⬦ reported, "The Prophet ⬦ said, 'The best place of worship for women is the [inner most] depth of their homes.'" (*Mustadrak ʿalā al-Ṣaḥīḥayn* 756)

During ṣalāh:

- You must recite Sūrat al-Fātiḥah[142] and a *sūrah*, or three short verses, or one lengthy verse in;

    (1) Both *rakaʿāt* of *Fajr*.

    (2) The first two *rakaʿāt* of *Ẓuhr*, *ʿAṣr*, *Maghrib* and *ʿIshāʾ*.

    (3) Every *rakʿah* of the *nafl* and *witr* prayers.

- You must recite the Qurʾān audibly in *Fajr*, *Maghrib* and *ʿIshāʾ*; and silently in *Ẓuhr* and *ʿAṣr* when leading a congregation.
- You must perform each posture calmly and properly.[143]
- You must sit after two *rakaʿāt* in a three or four *rakaʿāt* prayer.[144]

---

142 ʿUbādah ibn Ṣāmit ﵁ reported that Allāh's Messenger ﷺ said, "The *ṣalāh* of a person who fails to recite the opening [chapter] of [Allāh's] Book (i.e. Sūrat al-Fātiḥah) is not valid." (*Ṣaḥīḥ al-Bukhārī* 756)

143 Abū Hurayrah ﵁ reported, "Allāh's Messenger ﷺ entered the Masjid. A man then entered, performed *ṣalāh* and then greeted the Prophet ﷺ with *salām*. The Prophet ﷺ responded to the greeting and said, 'Go back and perform *ṣalāh*, for you did not perform *ṣalāh*.' The man then returned and performed *ṣalāh* just as he performed it [before]. After that he came and greeted the Prophet ﷺ with *salām*. The Prophet ﷺ responded three times, 'Go back and perform *ṣalāh*, for you did not perform *ṣalāh*.' The man then expressed, 'I swear by the One who has sent you with the truth, I cannot do better than this. Please teach me."

The Prophet ﷺ explained, 'When you stand to perform *ṣalāh* say *allāhuakbar*. Then recite whatever portion of the Qurʾān is easy for you, which you have [retained] with you. After that, go into *rukūʿ* until you are comfortably positioned in *rukūʿ*. Then get up and stand straight. Then go into *sajdah* until you are comfortably positioned in *sajdah*. After that, get up until you are comfortably positioned in a sitting position. Carry this out throughout your entire *ṣalāh*.'" (*Ṣaḥīḥ al-Bukhārī* 757)

144 ʿĀʾishah ﵂ reported, "Allāh's Messenger ﷺ [. . .] would say the *taḥīyah*

◇ You must recite the *taḥīyah* and the *tashahhud*.[145]

◇ You must perform every posture in the correct sequence.[146]

◇ You must immediately prostrate (*sujūd al-tilāwah*) upon reciting a prostration verse.[147]

◇ Before concluding the prayer you must prostrate twice (*sujūd al-sahw*) if you accidentally missed a *wājib* action or performed it out of its proper place during *ṣalāh*.[148]

Ending the ṣalāh:

◇ You must say *as-salāmu ʿalaykum wa raḥmatullāh* while turning your head to your right and then to your left.[149]

---

during the sitting [after] every two *rakaʿāt* [. . .]." (*Ṣaḥīḥ Muslim* 1110)

145 ʿAbdullāh ⬥ reported, "During *ṣalāh* we used to say [while sitting] behind Allāh's Messenger ﷺ, 'Peace be upon Allāh. Peace be upon so and so.' So Allāh's Messenger ﷺ told us one day, 'Allāh is peace. When any of you sit during *ṣalāh* he should say, 'Greetings are for Allāh, as well as prayers and all pure things. Peace be upon you, Prophet, along with Allāh's mercy and blessings. Peace be upon us and upon all of Allāh's righteous servants'—when he utters this, [its blessings] reaches every pious servant of Allāh within the heaven(s) and the earth—'I testify there is no God but Allāh and I testify that Muḥammad is Allāh's servant and messenger.' Then he may choose whatever request he would like [to make to Allāh].'" (*Ṣaḥīḥ Muslim* 897)

146 Refer to footnote 143

147 Ibn ʿUmar ⬥ reported, "Allāh's Messenger ﷺ used to recite the Qurʾān to us. When he would pass by a *sajdah* [verse during his recitation], he would say, '*Allāhu akbar*,' and prostrate. We would [also] prostrate with him." (*Sunan Abū Dāwūd* 1413)

148 Thawbān ⬥ reported, "The Prophet ﷺ said, 'For every mistake [made during *ṣalāh*] there are two prostrations [that are required to be made] after saying *salām*.'" (*Sunan Abū Dāwūd* 1038)

149 ʿAlī ⬥ reported, "The Prophet ﷺ said, 'The key to *ṣalāh* is [to attain] purity. The restrictions of *ṣalāh* (i.e. its opening) are [imposed] by saying *Allāhu akbar* and the removal of its restriction (i.e. its closing) is by saying *salām*.'" (*Jāmiʿ al-Tirmidhī* 3)

Note: After the *ṣalāh* you must say the *takbīr* during the days of *'Arafah*, *'Īd* and *Tashrīq*. The *takbīr* will begin from the *Fajr* of the 9th of *Dhū al-Ḥijjah* and end at the *'Aṣr* of the 13th.[150]

HOW DO I PERFORM *ṢALĀH* ACCORDING TO THE SUNNAH?

- Stand straight facing the *qiblah*.[151]
- Keep a gap of four fingers between your feet.
- Make an active intention in your heart to perform the *ṣalāh* you intend to carry out e.g. I intend to perform the *farḍ* prayer of *Fajr* for Allah's sake.[152]
- *Men*: Raise both hands up to your earlobes with your palms facing the *qiblah*.[153]
- *Women*: Raise both hands up to your shoulders with your palms facing the *qiblah*.[154]
- Say *Allāhu akbar*.[155]

---

150 "And remember Allāh during [specific] numbered days [. . .]."(Sūrat al-Baqarah 2:203)

151 "So turn your face toward Masjid al-Ḥarām. And wherever you may be, turn your faces toward it [in ṣalāh]." (Sūrat al-Baqarah 2:144)

152 'Umar ibn al-Khaṭṭāb ﷺ narrated, "I heard Allāh's Messenger ﷺ say, 'Deeds are solely dependent on intentions, and every person will receive what they intended [. . .].'" (*Ṣaḥīḥ al-Bukhārī* 1)

153 Anas ﷺ narrated, "I saw Allāh's Messenger ﷺ [say], '*Allāhu akbar*.' He made his thumbs parallel to his ears [. . .]." (*Mustadrak 'alā al-Ṣaḥīḥayn* 822)

154 'Abdullāh ibn 'Umar ﷺ reported that Allāh's Messenger ﷺ would raise his hands [until] they were parallel to his shoulders when he would begin *ṣalāh* [. . .]."(*Ṣaḥīḥ al-Bukhārī* 735)

155 Refer to footnote 149

- *Men*: Place your right palm over your left hand below your navel.[156]
- *Women*: Place your right palm over your left hand on your chest.
- Look toward the area where your forehead will rest during prostration.[157]
- Recite the praises of Allāh ﷻ (*thanā'*):

سُبْحَانَكَ اللّٰهُمَّ وَبِحَمْدِكَ وَتَبَارَكَ اسْمُكَ
وَتَعَالٰى جَدُّكَ وَلَا إِلٰـهَ غَيْرُكَ

Subḥānaka Allāhumma wa-bi-ḥamdika wa-ta-bāraka smuka wa-ta ʿālā jadduka wa-lā ilāha ghayruk.

Glory be to you O Allāh with Your praises. Your name is exalted and Your significance is transcendent. There is no god besides You.[158]

---

156 Hulb ﷺ reported, "Allāh's Messenger ﷺ used to lead us in prayer. He would take hold of his left hand with his right hand."

Abū ʿĪsā [al-Tirmidhī] said, "Hulb's ḥadīth is a reliable (*ḥasan*) *ḥadīth*. This is what is to be practiced according to scholars from the Prophet's companions, the *Tābiʿūn* and those who succeeded them. Their view is that a man should place his right hand over his left hand during *ṣalāh*. Some of them are of the opinion that he should place them both above the navel while others are of the opinion that he should place them both below the navel. Each one of these stances is acceptable according to them." (*Jāmiʿ al-Tirmidhī* 252)

ʿAlī ﷺ reported, "The *sunnah* is to place the palm over the palm below the navel during *ṣalāh*." (*Sunan Abū Dāwūd* 1413)

157 Anas ibn Mālik ﷺ reported, "Allāh's Messenger ﷺ said, 'What is wrong with [those] people who raise their gaze during their *ṣalāh*? This practice should definitely be stopped or else their eyesight will be taken away.'" (*Ṣaḥīḥ al-Bukhārī* 750)

Anas ﷺ reported, "Allāh's Messenger ﷺ said, 'Anas, place your gaze [at the area] where you will prostate.'" (*Sunan al-Kubrā al-Bayhaqī* 3545)

158 Abū Saʿīd ﷺ reported, "When the Prophet ﷺ would begin [his] *ṣalāh* he

◈ Recite the *taʿawwudh*:

أَعُوْذُ بِاللّٰهِ مِنَ الشَّيْطَانِ الـرَّجِيْمِ.

Aʿūdhu billāhi mina sh-Shayṭāni r-Rajīm.

I seek Allāh's protection from the
Satan who is banished.[159]

◈ Recite the *basmalah*;

بِسْمِ اللّٰهِ الـرَّحْمٰنِ الـرَّحِيْمِ.

Bismillāhi r-Raḥmāni r-Raḥīm.[160]

[I begin] with Allāh's name who is the
Most Merciful and the Ever Merciful.

◈ Recite *Sūrat al-Fātiḥah*,[161] the first chapter of the Qurʿān, when leading a congregation as an imam or performing *ṣalāh* individually. Otherwise remain silent.[162]

---

would say, 'Glory be to you O Allāh with Your praises. Your name is exalted and Your significance is transcendent. There is no god besides You.'" (*Sunan al-Nasaʾī* 900)

159 "So when you recite the Qur'an, [first] seek Allāh's refuge from the Satan who is banished [from Allāh's mercy]." (Sūrat al-Naḥl 16:98)

160 Ibn ʿAbbās ﷺ reported, "The Prophet ﷺ would begin his *ṣalāh* with, '[I begin] with the name of Allāh, the All Merciful, the Ever Merciful.'" (*Jāmiʿ al-Tirmidhī* 245)

161 ʿUbādah ibn Ṣāmit ﷺ reported that Allāh's Messenger ﷺ said, "The *ṣalāh* of a person who fails to recite the opening [chapter] of [Allāh's] Book (i.e. *Sūrat al-Fātiḥah*) is not valid." (*Ṣaḥīḥ al-Bukhārī* 756)

162 "So when the Qurʾān is recited, listen to it and pay attention so that you may receive [divine] mercy." (Sūrat al-Aʿrāf 7:204)

◇ Say '*āmīn*' once the recitation of Sūrat al-Fātiḥah is completed.[163]

◇ Recite:

(1) A complete *sūrah* or

(2) Three short verses or

(3) One lengthy verse when leading a congregation or performing *ṣalāh* individually.[164]

◇ Say '*Allāhu akbar*' and go into *rukū*ʿ[165] by bending your body in a 90 degree angle. Keep your back straight and your head levelled with your back.[166] Grip your knees with your palms and spread your fingers out. Fix your gaze on the area between your feet.[167]

◇ Recite the *tasbīḥ* three times:

سُبْحَانَ رَبِّيَ الْعَظِيمِ.

Subḥāna rabbiya l-ʿaẓīm.

---

163 Abū Hurayrah reported, "The Prophet said, 'When the imam says *āmīn*, you should say *āmīn*, for whoever's *āmīn* corresponds with the *āmīn* of the angels, all their past sins will be forgiven.'" (*Ṣaḥīḥ al-Bukhārī* 780)

164 Jābir ibn Samurah reported, "Allāh's Messenger would recite *wa s-samāʾi wa ṭ-ṭāriq, wa s-samāʾi dhāti l-burūj* and similar chapters [of the Qurʾān] during *Ẓuhr* and *ʿAṣr*." (*Sunan Abū Dāwūd* 805)

165 ʿAbdullāh ibn Masʿūd reported, "Allāh's Messenger would say, '*Allāhu akbar*,' every time [he would] go down, get up, stand and sit [during *ṣalāh*]. Abū Bakr and ʿUmar would do the same.'" (*Jāmiʿ al-Tirmidhī* 253)

166 Abū Masʿūd al-Badrī reported, "Allāh's Messenger said, 'The *ṣalāh* of a man is insufficient until he straightens his back during *rukū*ʿ and *sujūd*.'" (*Sunan Abū Dāwūd* 855)

167 Wāʾil reported, "Whenever the Prophet performed *rukū*ʿ he would spread out his fingers." (*Mustadrak ʿalā al-Ṣaḥīḥayn* 814)

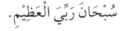

Glory be to my Sustainer, the Most Great.[168]

◇ Stand up straight while saying, '*sami' Allāhu li-man ḥam-idah*' (Allāh hears those who praise Him), provided you are leading a congregation or performing *ṣalāh* individually.[169]

◇ Say once:

$$\text{رَبَّنَا وَ لَكَ الْحَمْدُ.}$$

Rabbanā wa laka l-ḥamd.

Our Sustainer, all praise is for You.[170]

◇ Say '*Allāhu akbar*'[171] and go into *sujūd* by placing your knees on the ground first, then your hands, then your nose, and then finally your forehead.[172]

◇ *Men:* Keep your hands by your head[173] with your fingers

168 Ḥudhayfah ☙ reported that he prayed with the Prophet ﷺ. During his *rukū'* the Prophet ﷺ would say, 'Glory be to my Sustainer, the Most Great.' And during his *sujūd* [he would say], 'Glory be to my Sustainer, the Most High.' [. . .]." (*Sunan Abū Dāwūd* 871)

169 Abū Hurayrah ☙ reported, "Allāh's Messenger ﷺ said, 'When the imam says, 'Allāh hears those who praise him,' say, 'O Allāh, our Sustainer, all praise is for you.' Whoever's statement coincides with the angels' statement; all their past sins will be forgiven.'" (*Ṣaḥīḥ al-Bukhārī* 796)

170 ibid.

171 Refer to footnote 165

172 Wā'il ibn Ḥujar ☙ reported, "Whenever Allāh's Messenger ﷺ prostrated, I saw that he would place his knees [on the ground] before his hands. When he would get up, he would lift his hands before his knees." (*Jāmi' al-Tirmidhī* 268)

173 Abū Is'ḥāq reported, "I asked Barā' ibn 'Āzib ☙, 'Where would the Prophet ﷺ place his face when prostrating?' He replied, 'Between his hands.'" (*Jāmi' al-Tir-midhī* 271)

closed[174] and facing the *qiblah*. Keep your abdomen away from your thighs[175] and your arms raised from the ground away from your flanks.[176] Position your toes towards the *qiblah*.

◇ *Women*: Keep your hands by your shoulders with your fingers closed and facing the *qiblah*. Attach your abdomen to your thighs and rest your forearms on the ground keeping them attached to your flanks.[177]

◇ Recite the following *tasbīḥ* three times:

سُبْحَانَ رَبِّيَ الْأَعْلَى.

Subḥāna rabbiya l-aʿlā.

Glory be to my Sustainer, the Most High.[178]

---

174 Wā'il ﷺ reported, "The Prophet ﷺ would join his fingers when prostrating." (*Mustadrak ʿalā al-Ṣaḥīḥayn* 826)

175 Maymūnah, the Prophet's wife ﷺ reported, "Whenever the Prophet ﷺ prostrated, if a kid (baby goat) wanted to pass by beneath him, it would be able to pass." (*Ṣaḥīḥ Muslim* 1107)

176 Barā' ﷺ reported, "Allāh's Messenger ﷺ said, 'When you prostrate, place your palms [on the ground] and raise your elbows.'" (*Ṣaḥīḥ Muslim* 1104)

Anas ﷺ reported, "Allāh's Messenger ﷺ said, 'Be balanced in prostration. [While you're in it] none of you should spread your arms out [on the ground] like a dog.'" (*Ṣaḥīḥ Muslim* 1102)

Jaʿfar ibn Rabīʿah ﷺ reported, "Whenever Allāh's Messenger ﷺ prostrated, he would spread out his arms away from his armpits to the extent that I would be able to see the whiteness of his armpits." (*Ṣaḥīḥ Muslim* 1106)

177 ʿAbdullāh ibn ʿUmar ﷺ reported, "Allāh's Messenger ﷺ said, 'When a woman sits during *ṣalāh*, she will place [one of her] thighs above the other thigh. When she prostrates, she will attach her stomach to her thighs [in a manner that it] resemble the most concealing state of hers, for Allāh will look at her and say, 'My Angels, I make you all a witness that I have forgiven her."" (*Sunan al-Kubrā al-Bayhaqī* 3199)

178 Refer to footnote 168

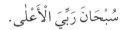

◇ Say '*Allāhu akbar*'[179] and sit up placing both hands on your thighs with the tips of your fingers touching the edge of your knees.

◇ *Men*: Sit on your left foot with your right foot propped up and its toes facing the *qiblah*.[180]

◇ *Women*: Sit on your left buttock placing your right thigh over your left thigh and have both feet extend to your right.[181]

◇ Say '*Allāhu akbar*' and go into *sujūd* as described before.[182]

◇ Say '*Allāhu akbar*' and stand from *sujūd* by raising your head followed by your hands and then your knees.[183]

◇ Repeat all procedures as previously explained for standing, *rukūʿ* and *sujūd* with the exception of reciting the *thanāʾ*, *taʿawwudh* and *basmalah*.

◇ Say '*Allāhu akbar*' and sit up as described for both men and women.

◇ Recite the *taḥīyah* and the *tashahhud*.

اَلتَّحِيَّاتُ لِلّٰهِ وَالصَّلَوَاتُ وَالطَّيِّبَاتُ السَّلَامُ عَلَيْكَ أَيُّهَا النَّبِيُّ

---

179 Refer to footnote 165

180 Wāʾil ibn Ḥujar ؓ reported, "I came to Madīnah [and] said [to myself], 'I will definitely watch the *ṣalāh* of Allāh's Messenger ﷺ. So when he sat i.e. for *tashahhud*, he spread his left foot out and placed his left hand on his left thigh, and propped up his right foot." (*Jāmiʿ al-Tirmidhī* 292)

181 Abū Ḥumayd ؓ reported, "I watched Allāh's Messenger ﷺ. When he would sit after two *rakaʿāt*, he would sit on the sole of his left foot and prop up the right foot. When it would be the fourth [*rakaʿāt*] he would connect his left buttock to the ground and would take his two feet out from one side." (*Sunan al-Kubrā al-Bayhaqī* 2773)

182 Refer to footnote 165

183 Refer to footnote 172

وَرَحْمَةُ اللّٰهِ وَبَرَكَاتُهُ السَّلَامُ عَلَيْنَا وَعَلَى عِبَادِ اللّٰهِ الصَّالِحِينَ
أَشْهَدُ أَنْ لَا إِلٰهَ إِلَّا اللّٰهُ وَأَشْهَدُ أَنَّ مُحَمَّدًا عَبْدُهُ وَرَسُوْلُهُ.

*At-taḥīyātu lillāhi wa ṣ-ṣalwātu wa ṭ-ṭayībātu s-salāmu ʿalayka
ayyuha n-nabīyu wa raḥmatullāhi wa barakātuhu s-salāmu
ʿalaynā wa ʿalā ʿibādi l-lāhi ṣ-ṣāliḥīn. Ash'hadu al-lā ilāha
illalāhu wa ash'hadu anna Muḥammadan ʿabduhū wa rasūluh.*

Greetings are for Allāh as well as prayers and all pure things.
Peace be upon you O Prophet, as well as Allāh's mercy and
blessings. Peace be upon us and upon Allāh's righteous
servants. I testify there is no God besides Allāh and I testify
that Muḥammad is Allāh's servant and messenger.[184]

◇ When reciting the *tashahhud* clasp the fingers of your right
hand and connect your thumb with your middle finger.
Raise your index finger so that it points to the *qiblah*.[185]

---

184 ʿAbdullāh ☙ reported, "During *ṣalāh* we used to say [while sitting] behind
Allāh's Messenger ☙, 'Peace be upon Allāh. Peace be upon so and so.' So Allāh's
Messenger ☙ told us one day, 'Allāh is peace. When any of you sit during *ṣalāh* you
should say, 'Greetings are for Allāh as well as prayers and all pure things. Peace be
upon you, Prophet, along with Allāh's mercy and blessings. Peace be upon us and
upon Allāh's righteous servants'—when he utters this, [its effect] reaches every pious
servant of Allāh in the heaven[s] and the earth—'I testify there is no God besides Allāh
and I testify that Muḥammad is Allāh's servant and messenger.' Then he may choose
whatever request he would like [to make to Allāh].'" (*Ṣaḥīḥ Muslim* 897)

185 Wā'il ibn Ḥujar ☙ reported, "I said [to myself], 'I will definitely watch
the *ṣalāh* of Allāh's Messenger ☙; how does he pray?'" [. . .] "Then he sat down. He
spread his left foot out and placed his left hand on his left thigh. He kept his right
elbow on his right thigh. He made a fist out of two fingers (i.e. the pinkie and the ring
finger) and made a ring [out of the middle finger and the thumb] saying such and such."
Bishr [the sub-narrator demonstrated this by making] a ring shape out of his
thumb and middle finger. He pointed [to the *qiblah*] using his index finger." (*Sunan
Abū Dāwūd* 957)

After the *tashahhud*, lower your index finger slightly and then keep it in that position until the end of the prayer.[186]

◇ If your prayer consists of three or four *rakaʿāt*, then stand up after completing the *tashahhud*[187] and carry out the remaining *rakaʿāt* as described before. If your *ṣalāh* is not a *farḍ* one, then add a *sūrah* after reciting *Sūrat al-Fātiḥah*.[188] If it is a farḍ one, suffice with reciting *Sūrat al-Fātiḥah* and then go into *rukūʿ*.

◇ If the sitting is the final one of the prayer then recite the following *ṣalawāt* after the *tashahhud*.[189]

---

186 Numayr 🕮 reported that he watched Allāh's Messenger 🕮 sit during *ṣalāh*. He placed his right arm on his right thigh and raised his index finger. He curved it slightly while he supplicated." (*Sunan al-Nasaʾī* 1275)

187 ʿĀʾishah 🕮 reported, "Allāh's Messenger 🕮 would not [recite anything] more than the *tashahhud* [while sitting after performing] two *rakaʿāt*." (*Majmaʿ al-Zawāʾid* 2859)

188 Abū Qatādah 🕮 reported, "The Prophet 🕮 would recite the 'Mother of the Book' (i.e. *Sūrat al-Fātiḥah*) and two *surahs* in the first two *rakaʿāt* of *ẓuhr* and [only] the 'Mother of the Book' in the last two *rakaʿāt*. [. . .]." (*Ṣaḥīḥ al-Bukhārī* 776)

[Imām] Muḥammad [ibn Ḥasan al-Shaybānī] stated, "The *sunnah* is that the opening chapter of the Book (i.e. *Sūrat al-Fātiḥah*) and a *surah* be recited during the first two *rakaʿāt* of a *farḍ* prayer. During the last two *rakaʿāt* [simply recite] the opening chapter of the Book. If you [decide] not to recite [*Sūrat al-Fātiḥah*] in them [and rather remain silent], this will be sufficient for you. If you [instead] say *subḥān'Allāh* in them, this will also be sufficient for you. This is the view of Imām Abū Ḥanīfah. (*Muʿaṭṭa li-Imām Muḥammad* 133)

189 ʿAbd al-Raḥmān ibn Abū Laylah 🕮 reported, "Kaʿb ibn ʿUjrah 🕮 met me and proposed, 'Can I not give you a gift? The Prophet 🕮 [once] came out to us so we asked him, 'Messenger of Allāh, we are aware of how to greet you, how are we supposed to pray for you?' He replied, 'Say, 'O Allāh, bless Muḥammad and the family of Muḥammad just as you blessed the family of Ibrāhīm. Truly you are the Most Praiseworthy and Noble. O Allāh, favour Muḥammad and the family of Muḥammad just as you favoured the family of Ibrāhīm. Truly you are the Most Praiseworthy and Noble.'" (*Ṣaḥīḥ al-Bukhārī* 6357)

اَللّٰهُمَّ صَلِّ عَلٰى مُحَمَّدٍ وَّعَلٰى اٰلِ مُحَمَّدٍ كَمَا صَلَّيْتَ عَلٰى اٰلِ إِبْرَاهِيْمَ إِنَّكَ حَمِيْدٌ مَجِيْدٌ. اللّٰهُمَّ بَارِكْ عَلٰى مُحَمَّدٍ وَّعَلٰى اٰلِ مُحَمَّدٍ كَمَا بَارَكْتَ عَلٰى اٰلِ إِبْرَاهِيْمَ إِنَّكَ حَمِيْدٌ مَجِيْدٌ.

Allāhumma ṣalli ʿalā Muḥammadin wa ʿalā Āli Muḥammadin kamā ṣallayta ʿalā Āli Ibrāhīma innaka Ḥamīdu m-Majīd. Allāhumma bārik ʿalā Muḥammadin wa ʿalā' Āli Muḥammadin kamā bārakta ʿalā Āli Ibrāhīma innaka Ḥamīdu m-Majīd.

O Allāh, bless Muḥammad and the family of Muḥammad just as you blessed the family of Ibrāhīm. Truly you are the Most Praiseworthy and Noble. O Allāh, favour Muḥammad and the family of Muḥammad just as you favoured the family of Ibrāhīm. Truly you are the Most Praiseworthy and Noble.

- Conclude your *ṣalāh* with a supplication (*du'ā'*) that has been mentioned in the Qur'ān or *ḥadīth*.[190]
- Say '*as-salāmu ʿalaykum wa-raḥmatullāh*' while turning your head to the right and look at your shoulder. Then say it a second time while turning your head to the left and look at your shoulder.[191]

---

190 Abū Bakr al-Ṣiddīq ✽ reported that he asked Allāh's Messenger ✽, "Teach me a supplication that I can make during my *ṣalāh*." He said, "Say, 'O Allāh, I have wronged myself greatly and only you forgive sins, so provide me with forgiveness on your behalf and have mercy on me. You are the All Forgiving and the Ever Merciful.'" (*Ṣaḥīḥ al-Bukhārī* 834)

191 ʿAbdullāh ✽ reported that the Prophet ✽ used to say *salām* on his right [side] and left [side, with the words], 'May peace and Allāh's mercy be unto you.'" (*Jāmiʿ al-Tirmidhī* 295)

WHAT ACTIONS ARE *MAKRŪH* DURING *ṢALĀH*?

◇ To do anything against the *sunnah* of *ṣalāh*.

◇ To pray in an area where pictures or portraits of animate objects are hung.[192]

◇ For the imam or some of his followers to stand on a raised platform while others are on lower ground.

◇ For a latecomer to proceed into *rukū'* before reaching a row of the congregational prayer.[193]

◇ To not join any row of congregants despite space being available and instead pray individually in a separate row.[194]

◇ To lean on something while standing.

◇ To keep your hair braided, if you're a male.[195]

◇ To pray topless, if you're a male.[196]

---

192 'Abdullāh ibn 'Umar ❧ reported, "Jibrīl promised [to meet] the Prophet ﷺ [at a particular time but failed to show up. Later] Jibrīl explained, 'We do not enter a house that has an image or a dog [in it].'" (*Ṣaḥīḥ al-Bukhārī* 3227)

193 Abū Bakrah ❧ reported that he reached the Prophet ﷺ [at the Masjid] while the Prophet ﷺ was in *rukū'*. As a result, Abū Bakrah performed *rukū'* before reaching the row. He later mentioned this to the Prophet ﷺ. The Prophet ﷺ expressed, "May Allāh increases your aspiration [to join the prayer quickly, however] do not do this again." (*Ṣaḥīḥ al-Bukhārī* 783)

194 Wābiṣah ibn Ma'bad ❧ reported that a man performed *ṣalāh* individually behind the row [where the other congregants were standing]. So the Prophet ﷺ instructed him to repeat his *ṣalāh*." (*Jāmi' al-Tirmidhī* 231)

195 Abū Sa'd, a resident of Madīnah reported, "I saw Abū Rāfi' [. . .] watch Ḥasan ibn 'Alī ❧, who was praying. Ḥasan had his hair braided so Abū Rāfi' [went over and] untied it [. . .] and explained, 'Allāh's Messenger ﷺ forbade men from praying with their hair braided.'" (*Sunan Ibn Mājah* 1042)

196 Abū Hurayrah ❧ reported, "Allāh's Messenger ﷺ said, 'None of you

- To place a cloth, such as a shawl, over your head or shoulders in a manner that its corners dangle down.[197]
- To wear clothing which you would not wear in the presence of a respectable person.
- To fiddle with your clothes or any part of your body.[198]
- To hold back your clothes.[199]
- To keep your mouth covered.[200]
- To spit or clean out your nose.[201]
- To blow air from your mouth.
- To keep your eyes shut.

---

should pray in only one garment in a manner that no portion of it is covering your shoulders.'" (*Ṣaḥīḥ al-Bukhārī* 359)

197 Abū Hurayrah reported, "Allāh's Messenger forbade [us from] hanging any clothing [on our body] during *ṣalāh*. [He also disapproved of] men covering their mouths [during *ṣalāh*]." (*Sunan Abū Dāwūd* 643)

198 Abū Hurayrah reported, "Allāh's Messenger said, 'Truly, a repulsive act is that a man wipes his forehead repeatedly before concluding his *ṣalāh*.'" (*Sunan Ibn Mājah* 964)

199 Ibn 'Abbās reported, "The Prophet said, 'I have been instructed to prostrate on seven bones (i.e. to connect seven parts of my body to the ground) and to not hold back any [part of my] clothing and hair [during *ṣalāh*].'" (*Ṣaḥīḥ Muslim* 1096)

200 Refer to footnote 197

201 Anas ibn Mālik reported, "Allāh's Messenger said, 'When you are [occupied] in *ṣalāh*, you are having a private dialogue with your Sustainer. Hence, none of you should ever spit [in the direction] that is in front of you or on your right side. Rather [if you really need to spit, you may spit] on your left hand side or below your feet.'" (*Ṣaḥīḥ Muslim* 1230)

It should be noted that in those days the masjid was uncarpeted and the ground was of sand and dirt. Therefore, this instruction could easily be applied in that environment. In this day and age where the masjids are primarily carpeted, one should avoid even attempting to spit in any area of the masjid let alone do it.

- To look around.[202]
- To wipe dust or sweat off your forehead.[203]
- To stretch and yawn.[204]
- To interlock the fingers of both hands.
- To crack your fingers.[205]
- To count verses of the Qur'ān or *tasbīḥ* (words of glorification) using your fingers.
- To place your hands on your hips.[206]
- To perform *rukūʿ* or *sujūd* before the imam.[207]
- To recite the Qur'ān in a posture other than *qiyām* (standing).[208]

---

202 Abū Dharr ﵁ reported, "Allāh's Messenger ﷺ said, 'Allāh, the Great and Almighty continues to pay attention to [His] servant while [His servant] is occupied in *ṣalāh*, as long as the servant does not look here and there. When he looks around, Allāh turns away from him.'" (*Sunan Abū Dāwūd* 909)

203 Refer to footnote 198

204 Abū Saʿīd al-Khudrī ﵁ reported, "Allāh's Messenger ﷺ said, 'When any of you yawn during *ṣalāh*, you should suppress it as much as you can, for truly Shaytān enters [your mouth at that time].'" (*Ṣaḥīḥ Muslim* 7492)

205 ʿAlī ﵁ reported Allāh's Messenger ﷺ said, "Do not crack your fingers while in *ṣalāh*." (*Sunan Ibn Mājah* 965)

206 Abū Hurayrah ﵁ reported, "Men have been forbidden from putting their hands on their waist [during *ṣalāh*].'" (*Ṣaḥīḥ al-Bukhārī* 1220)

207 Abū Hurayrah ﵁ reported, "Muḥammad ﷺ said, 'Does the person who raises their head before the imam not fear that Allāh may transform their head into the head of a donkey?'" (*Ṣaḥīḥ Muslim* 963)

208 ʿAlī ibn Abū Ṭālib ﵁ reported, "Allāh's Messenger ﷺ forbade me from reciting the Qur'ān while in *rukūʿ* and *sujūd*." (*Ṣaḥīḥ Muslim* 1077)

- To wipe away pebbles or any other unharmful objects more than once from the area where you plans to prostrate.[209]
- To spread your forearms on the ground while prostrating.[210]
- To squat.[211]
- To sit cross legged without a reasonable excuse.[212]

WHAT ACTIONS INVALIDATE *ṢALĀH*?

- To deliberately break *wuḍū'*.[213]
- To speak on purpose or by mistake.[214]

---

209 Muʿayqīb reported, "Allāh's Messenger said about the person who levels the dirt in the area where they [plans to] prostrate, 'If he is going to do it, then [he should do it only] once.'" (*Ṣaḥīḥ Muslim* 1222)

210 Anas reported, "Allāh's Messenger said, 'Excercise a moderate [pace] during prostration. None of you should spread your arms out [in prostration] like [that of] a dog [. . .].'" (*Ṣaḥīḥ al-Bukhārī* 532)

211 ʿAlī reported, "Allāh's Messenger told me, "Alī, I like for you whatever I like for myself and I dislike for you whatever I dislike for myself; do not squat between the two prostrations.'" (*Jāmiʿ al-Tirmidhī* 282)

212 ʿAbdullāh ibn ʿUmar reported that he saw his father [ʿUmar sitting] cross-legged during *ṣalāh* [due to a certain medical condition]. ʿAbdullāh reports, "So I did the same. I was young during those days. My father then forbade me from doing so and explained, 'This is not the *sunnah* of *ṣalāh*. The *sunnah* of *ṣalāh* is that you prop up your right foot and fold your left foot [when sitting].'" (*Muʿaṭṭa li-Imām Muḥammad* 151)

213 ʿĀ'ishah narrated that the Prophet said, "Whoever vomits, has a nosebleed, a reflux or some pre-seminal discharge [while performing *ṣalāh*], should turn away [from *ṣalāh*] and perform *wuḍū'*." (*Sunan Ibn Mājah* 1221)

214 Muʿāwiyah ibn al-Ḥakam al-Sulamī reported, "While I was [once] praying with Allāh's Messenger, a man from the community suddenly sneezed. I uttered [to him], 'May Allāh have mercy on you.' [The remainder of the] people began staring at me, so I said, 'O my mother's bereavement, what is wrong with you [all]. You're [all] looking at me [in such a repulsive manner]!' They then began striking their

- To respond to someone sneezing, greeting or speaking.[215]
- To articulate something that resembles human speech, such as saying 'ah', 'oh' or 'uff'.[216]
- To blow in a manner that a sound is heard.[217]
- To cough or clear the throat unnecessarily.
- To cry or express agony over something that is not connected to any part of your *ṣalāh*.
- To accept a correction in the recitation of the Qur'ān from someone who is not performing the same *ṣalāh* as you.
- To make an error in the recitation of the Qur'ān that distorts its meaning.
- To recite the Qur'ān by looking into a copy of it.
- To laugh aloud during *ṣalāh*.[218]

---

hands on their thighs. When I noticed that they were trying to silence me [I became angry] however I remained silent. When Allāh's Messenger ﷺ completed the prayer; I swear by my father and mother, I have never seen a teacher before him nor after him who taught better than him. By Allāh, he neither scolded me nor struck me nor insulted me. He [simply] expressed, 'No form of people's speech is appropriate in this prayer. [This prayer] is [simply a combination of] *tasbīḥ* (Allāh's glorification), *takbīr* (declaring Allāh's greatness) and the recitation of the Qur'ān.'" (*Ṣaḥīḥ Muslim* 1199)

215 ibid.

216 ibid.

217 Abū Ṣāliḥ ؓ reported, "I was with Umm Salamah ؓ when a relative of hers, who was a young man with hair that exceeded his earlobes, paid her a visit. He began praying and blew. Umm Salamah said, "My beloved son, do not blow, for I heard Allāh's Messenger ﷺ [once] say [in admonishment] to a black slave of ours [who was blowing in *ṣalāh*], 'Rabāḥ, may your face be covered in dirt. [What are you doing?]'" (*Sunan al-Kubrā al-Bayhaqī* 3363)

218 Abū Mūsā ؓ said, "[Once] while the Prophet ﷺ led people in *ṣalāh*, a man entered [the masjid] and fell into a well that was in the masjid. He had poor eyesight.

- To turn your chest away from the *qiblah*.
- To expose your *ʿawrah*.
- To carry out an action during *ṣalāh* which either involves using both hands or leaves an onlooker under the impression that you are not performing *ṣalāh*.
- To have a woman stand beside a man while performing the same congregational *ṣalāh*.
- To eat or drink during *ṣalāh*.

APART FROM THE *FARḌ* PRAYERS WHAT ELSE SHOULD I PERFORM?

There are 12 *rakaʿāt* you should perform throughout the day in addition to your *farḍ* prayers. These prayers have been classified as *Sunnat al-Muʾakkadah*:

- Two *rakaʿāt* before the *farḍ ṣalāh* of *Fajr*.[219]
- Four *rakaʿāt* before the *farḍ ṣalāh* of *Ẓuhr and Jumuʿah*.[220]

Many people laughed while they were performing *ṣalāh*. [Upon concluding the prayer] Allāh's Messenger ﷺ instructed [all] those who laughed to repeat their *wuḍūʾ* and to repeat their *ṣalāh*." (*Majmaʿ al-Zawāʾid* 1278)

219 ʿĀʾishah ﵂ reported, "Allāh's Messenger ﷺ would pray 13 *rakaʿāt* during the night. After that, he would pray two short *rakaʿāt* when he heard the call to *Ṣalāt al-Fajr*." (*Ṣaḥīḥ al-Bukhārī* 1170)

220 ʿAbdullāh ibn al-Sāʾib ﵁ reported, "Allāh's Messenger ﷺ would perform four *rakaʿāt* after the sun had moved [from its zenith] before performing *Ẓuhr*. He explained, 'This is an hour when the doors of the sky are opened. I would like a good deed of mine to ascend through them.'" (*Jāmiʿ al-Tirmidhī* 478)

- Two *raka'āt* after the *farḍ ṣalāh* of *Ẓuhr and Jumu'ah.*[221]
- Two *raka'āt* after the *farḍ ṣalāh* of *Maghrib.*[222]
- Two *raka'āt* after the *farḍ ṣalāh* of *'Ishā'*.[223]

Beyond these prayers there are four *raka'āt* you should perform which have been classified as *Sunnat Ghayr al-Mu'akkadah*:

- Four *raka'āt* before the *farḍ ṣalāh* of *'Aṣr.*[224]

221 Ibn 'Umar ﷺ reported, "I performed two *raka'āt* with the Prophet ﷺ before *Ẓuhr* and two *raka'āt* after *Ẓuhr*." (*Jāmi' al-Tirmidhī* 425)

222 Ibn 'Umar ﷺ reported, "I performed two *raka'āt* with the Prophet ﷺ after *Maghrib* at his house." (*Jāmi' al-Tirmidhī* 432)

223 'Abdullāh ibn Shaqīq ﷺ reported, "I asked 'Ā'ishah ﷺ about the [voluntary (*nafl*)] prayer of Allāh's Messenger ﷺ, so she explained, 'He used to perform two *raka'āt* before *Ẓuhr* and two *raka'āt* after it, two *raka'āt* after *Maghrib*, two *raka'āt* after *'Ishā'*, and two *raka'āt* before *Fajr*.'" (*Jāmi' al-Tirmidhī* 436)

224 Ibn 'Umar ﷺ reported, "The Prophet ﷺ said, 'May Allāh have mercy on the person who performs four [*raka'āt*] before *'Asr*.'" (*Jāmi' al-Tirmidhī* 430)

Wealth Purification

(*Zakāh*)

WHY IS PURIFYING MY WEALTH (*ZAKĀH*) IMPORTANT?

Zakāh is among the integral practices of Islam.[225] It brings tremendous benefits to the person who pays it regularly. For example:

⬦ It repels Allāh's anger.[226]

⬦ It absolves you from sin.[227]

⬦ It increases the blessings (*barakah*) in the remainder of your wealth.[228]

⬦ It is a means of being admitted into Paradise (*Jannah*).[229]

WHO MUST PAY *ZAKĀH*?

You must pay *zakāh* if you are:

---

225 Ibn 'Umar ❁ related, "Allāh's Messenger ❁ said, "Islam is built on five [pillars]:
• To testify (*shahādah*) that there is no god except Allāh and Muḥammad is the messenger of Allāh
• To establish ritual prayer (*ṣalāh*)
• To purify [your] wealth (*zakāh*)
• To go for pilgrimage (*ḥajj*)
• And to fast (*ṣawm*) during *Ramaḍān*.'" (*Ṣaḥīḥ al-Bukhārī* 8)

226 Anas ❁ reported, "Allāh's Messenger ❁ said, 'Verily charity estinguishes the anger of the Sustainer (*Rabb*) and repels an unpleasent death.'" (*Jāmiʿ al-Tirmidhī* 664)

227 "Take charity (*ṣadaqah*) from their wealth in order that it purify them [from sin] [. . .]." (Sūrat al-Tawbah 103)

228 "And whatever interest you give to [produce an] increase in people's wealth, it will not increase with Allāh. But whatever zakāh you give, desiring the countenance of Allāh—those are the multipliers." (Sūrat al-Rūm 39)

229 "Those who spend their wealth during the night and day, secretly and publicly, for them is their reward with their Sustainer (*Rabb*). And they will have no fear nor will they grieve." (Sūrat al-Baqarah 274)

- A Muslim.
- An adolescent (*bāligh*).[230]
- Sane.[231]
- Free of slavery.
- Acquainted with the obligation of *zakāh*.
- The complete owner and possessor of such wealth that is;
    (1) In excess of your basic needs
    (2) Beyond the minimum amount for you to be required to pay *zakāh* (*niṣāb*)
    (3) Free from such debt that is equal or more than the capital currently in your possession.
    (4) Productive, whether intrinsically, such as gold and silver or physically such as breeding or accumulating profits.

---

230 'Ā'ishah ﵂ reported, "Allāh's Messenger ﷺ said, 'The pen [used for documenting people's deeds] has been uplifted from [recording the actions of] three [types of people];

- A sleeping person, until they wake up
- A child, until he becomes mature (*bāligh*)
- A [person who is] mentally challenged, until they begin to understand or regain their sanity.'" (*Sunan Ibn Mājah* 2041)

According to Sacred Law (*sharī'ah*) you become mature either by turning 15 years of age in lunar years, or;

- (Male): You have a wet dream before turning 15.
- (Female): You have your menses or a wet dream before turning 15.

231 ibid.

WHAT AM I SUPPOSED TO PAY *ZAKĀH* ON?

You must pay *zakāh* on:

◇ Gold[232]

◇ Silver[233]

◇ Inventory[234]

◇ Cash savings

◇ Investments

◇ Camels[235]

---

232 Ibn 'Umar and 'Ā'ishah l reported, "The Prophet 繠 would take half a dinar (a gold coin) [for *zakāh*] from every 200 dinars or more [which a person had]. He would take a dinar from every 40 dinars [that a person had above the 200 mark]." (*Sunan Ibn Mājah* 1791)

233 'Alī 繠 reported, "The Prophet 繠 said, 'When you have 200 dirhams (silver coins) and a year passes by [with them being in your ownership and possession] then five dirhams are due on them [for *zakāh* at the completion of the year] [. . .].'" (*Sunan Abū Dāwūd* 1573)

234 Samurah ibn Jundub 繠 reported, "[. . .] Allāh's Messenger 繠 used to instruct us to take out *ṣadaqah* (i.e. *zakāh*) from the items we prepared for selling." (*Sunan Abū Dāwūd* 1562)

235 Anas 繠 reported that Abū Bakr 繠 wrote this document out for him when he was sending him to Bahrain:

"[I begin] with the name of Allāh who is Entirely Merciful and Especially Merciful. These [are the details of] the [divine] instructions on charity which Allāh's Messenger 繠 made obligatory on all Muslims; the very rules Allāh provided His Messenger with. Whichever Muslim is asked to pay it accordingly, they should pay. Whoever is asked to pay more should not pay [more].

For every 24 camels and less [*zakāh* will be paid] with sheep; for every 5 camels one sheep will be paid. When the [number of camels in one's ownership] reaches 25 to 35 then a one-year-old she-camel will be given. When [the number] reaches 36 to 45 then a two-year-old she-camel must be paid. When it reaches 46 to 60 then a three-year-old she camel must be paid. When it reaches 61 to 75 then a four-year-old she-camel must be paid. When it reaches 76 to 90 then 2 two-year-old she-camels

- Cows[236]
- Sheep and goats[237]
- Horses[238]
- Produce[239]

Zakāh is not due on home(s), household items, vehicle(s), clothing, collectable items, memorabilia and precious stones.

---

must be paid. When it reaches 91 to 120 then 2 three-year-old she-camels must be paid. If [the number] exceeds 120 then for every 40 [camels] a two-year-old she-camel will be paid and for every 50 a three-year-old she-camel will be paid.

Whoever has only 4 camels, there is no *ṣadaqah* (i.e. *zakāh*) that is to be paid on them except if their owner wishes [to pay voluntarily]. When the number of camels will reach 5 then a sheep will be paid on them.

Regarding *ṣadaqah* (i.e. *zakāh*) on sheep in a flock, if there are between 40 to 120, then a sheep [will be paid] on them. When their number exceeds 120 up to 200 then two sheep [will be paid on them]. When it exceeds 200 up to 300 then three sheep [will be paid] on them. If it exceeds 300 then for every 100 [sheep] a sheep [will be paid out].

If a person's flock happens to be less then forty by [even] one then there will be no *ṣadaqah* (i.e. *zakāh*) [due on them] except if their owner wishes [to pay voluntarily] [. . .]." (*Ṣaḥīḥ al-Bukhārī* 1454)

236 Muʿādh ibn Jabal ﷺ reported, "The Prophet ﷺ sent me to Yemen [as a governor] and instructed me to take [from its residents] a one-year-old male or female cow for every 30 cows [a person owned, for *zakāh* purposes] and a two-year-old cow from every 40 cows [. . .]." (*Jāmiʿ al-Tirmidhī* 623)

237 Please refer to footnote no. 235

238 Jābir ﷺ reported, "Allāh's Messenger ﷺ said, 'A dinar is due [for *zakāh*] on every type of grazing horse [a person owns].'" (*Sunan al-Kubrā al-Bayhaqī* 7419)

239 ʿAbdullāh ibn ʿUmar ﷺ reported, "The Prophet ﷺ said, 'One-tenth [of the produce that is grown and harvested] from a land that is irrigated by rain and springs, or from a land that is [naturally] wet, [must be paid in *zakāh*]. Whichever [land] is irrigated by a waterwheel, then half of one-tenth [of its produce must be given in *zakāh*].'" (*Ṣaḥīḥ al-Bukhārī* 1483)

WHEN DO I PAY *ZAKĀH* ON MY GOLD?

Zakāh must be paid on every gold item in your ownership and possession, irrespective of whether it is for personal use or not, such as gold nuggets, biscuits, jewellery etc. when it exceeds 87.84 grams / 2.82 troy ounces and has been in your possession for a complete lunar year. Upon the completion of the lunar year you must pay 2.5% of the total gold in *zakāh* either from the actual gold itself or its equal value in cash.

WHEN DO I PAY *ZAKĀH* ON MY SILVER?

Zakāh must be paid on every silver item in your ownership and possession when it exceeds 612.36 grams / 19.6 troy ounces and has been in your possession for a complete lunar year. Upon the completion of the lunar year you must pay 2.5% of the total silver in *zakāh* either from the actual silver itself or its equal value in cash.[240]

WHEN DO I PAY *ZAKĀH* ON MY INVENTORY?

As a business owner, you will calculate the value of your total inventory according to its current retail price in your local currency and see whether its value reaches the *niṣāb* of gold or silver. If it reaches the *niṣāb* of both gold and silver, you will calculate the *zakāh* that is due based on each value. Whichever amount yields more *zakāh,* you will pay accordingly in order to maximize the benefit to the needy.

240 To find out the current price of gold or silver please visit http://goldprice.org.

Note: If during the lunar year the value of your inventory falls below the *niṣāb*, however before the year is complete, it surpasses the *niṣāb* once again, this will not require you to restart the lunar year from the day the value surpassed the *niṣāb*. Rather, the original cycle will be completed.

WHEN DO I PAY *ZAKĀH* ON MY CASH SAVINGS?

Zakāh must be paid on the excess cash in your account provided it is equal or exceeds the *niṣāb* of silver and is held for a complete lunar year.

HOW DO I PAY *ZAKĀH* ON MY INVESTMENTS?

Stocks and Shares

If you purchase stocks or shares with the intention of actively trading them, then you will pay *zakāh* on the market value of your shares. If however you purchase the stocks or shares for earning dividends and to hold on to them for a long period of time then you will pay *zakāh* on the dividends and the market value of your share of the corporation's inventory. All the required information can be found on the financial statements of the corporation.

RRSP (Registered Retirement Savings Plan)

You will pay *zakāh* on the complete balance of your account one year after the amount has reached the *niṣāb*. Although some scholars have suggested that when calculating the *zakāh* on the balance, you may minus the tax you would have had to pay if you were to cash out the funds on the very day you plan to pay *zakāh*, the dominant view is that you must pay *zakāh* on the entire amount and not deduct a single penny.

RESP (Registered Education Savings Plan)

Since RESP's are invested for your children's post-secondary education and are registered under their name, there is no *zakāh* that is due on them as long as you have no intention of withdrawing the funds at any time prior to your child making the decision to pursue post-secondary education or not. However, if the investment exceeds the *niṣāb* and your child becomes mature (*bāligh*), they will have to pay *zakāh* on the investment. They can either pay the annual due on the yearly bases or defer it until the investment matures and then pay the total amount that was due on them ever since they became *bāligh*.

Note:

- If an investment is made in an Islamically impermissible source e.g. ale manufacturers, the entertainment industry, etc. or if the investment is interest bound e.g. bonds, then *zakāh* will be calculated on the initial investment and the profit accumulated from the investment, and will be given to the recipients of *zakāh* without expecting any reward from Allāh ﷻ.
- If the investment is made in a permissible source then *zakāh* will be calculated on the current market value of the investment.

For details on *zakāh* upon camels, cows, sheep, goats, horses and produce please refer to *Mukhtaṣar al-Qudūrī* or *Nūr al-Iḍāḥ* or contact your local scholar.

Dues and Debts

Technically a 'due' is of three categories:

- Strong: Money that is owed due to a commercial sale. In such circumstances the person who is owed money will calculate the *zakāh* that is to be paid on that due and will then pay it as they receive the funds.
- Medium: Money that is owed due to rendering a service. In this instance the person who is owed money will only pay *zakāh* on the due after they receive an amount that is equal to the *niṣāb* of silver and they hold on to it for a complete lunar year.
- Weak: Dues that are owed due to any other reason apart from the aforementioned two e.g. inheritance, marital gift (*mahr*) etc. *Zakāh* will be paid on this due once it is completely received and a lunar year passes while it remains in the owner's possession.

Technically a debt is of two types:

- Short term: when the total amount is to be paid on a specified date within the year.
- Long term: when the amount is to be paid at a later period and can be paid in instalments

If you incur a short term debt and the amount is equal or greater than your 'zakātable' assets, then no *zakāh* is due on you. If it is less, then the amount of the debt will be deducted and *zakāh* will be paid on the difference, provided the difference is equal or exceeds the *niṣāb*. In the case of long-term debts, such as bank-loans and vehicle financing, the payment of the month will only be deducted and *zakāh* will be paid on the difference.

WHEN WILL I PAY MY *ZAKĀH*?

You must pay *zakāh* if you have the *niṣāb* of any one of the aforementioned items and one lunar year has passed from the day you reached the *niṣāb*.[241] You will calculate the *zakāh* on the complete value of the item and not simply on what exceeds the *niṣāb*.

WHO DO I HAVE TO PAY MY *ZAKĀH* TO?

Allāh ﷻ has declared in verse 60 of Sūrat al-Tawbah, "*Zakāh is only for*;

- *The poor*—a person who does not have the *niṣāb* of any asset.
- *The needy*—a person who has nothing to their name.
- *Those employed to collect [zakāh]*—by an agency that is appointed by the authorities of a sovereign Islamic State.
- *Bringing [people's] hearts together [for Islam]*—this is not applicable today.
- *Freeing captives [or slaves]*.

241 Ibn 'Umar ؓ reported, "Allāh's Messenger ﷺ said, 'There is no *zakāh* [due] on a person's assets until a year passes.'" (*Sunan al-Dārquṭnī* 1970)

- *Those in debt,*
- *The cause of Allāh*—pilgrims who have become separated from their group and are unable to rejoin them without funds and for soldiers on an Islamic military campaign who have become detached from their unit and are unable to reconnect with them without funds.
- *The [stranded] traveler*—who does not possess the necessary means to reach home."

You will give *zakāh* to people from the aforementioned categories provided they are;

- Muslim.[242]
- Not your spouse.
- Not your descendant, or ancestor whether paternal or maternal.
- Not from the clan of Banū Hāshim i.e. the descendants of ʿAlī ibn Abū Ṭālib ﷺ, Jaʿfar ibn Abū Ṭālib ﷺ, ʿAbbās ibn Abd al-Muṭṭalib ﷺ, ʿAqīl ibn Abū Ṭālib and Ḥārith ibn Abū Ṭālib.[243]

---

242 Ibn ʿAbbās ﷺ reported, "The Prophet ﷺ sent Muʿādh ﷺ to Yemen and told him, 'Invite people to testify that there is no god except Allāh and that I am the Messenger of Allāh. If they listen [to you], then inform them that Allāh has obligated five ritual prayers on them for every morning and evening. If they obey this then tell them that Allāh has made an expense (*zakāh*) mandatory on their [surplus] assets which will be taken from their rich and given to their poor.'" (*Ṣaḥīḥ al-Bukhārī* 1395)

243 ʿAbd al-Muṭṭalib ibn Rabīʿah and Faḍl ibn ʿAbbās ﷺ reported, "[. . .] The Prophet ﷺ then told us, 'These donations are people's rubbish. It is neither permissible for Muḥammad nor for Muḥammad's family [. . .].'" (*Ṣaḥīḥ Muslim* 2482)

Fasting (*Ṣawm*) During Ramaḍān

WHAT IS FASTING (*ṢAWM*)?

Ṣawm is defined as 'to intentionally not eat, drink and have sex from dawn to sunset.'[244]

WHY IS *ṢAWM* IMPORTANT?

Ṣawm is an integral practice of Islam.[245] It is an activity that yields great benefits. For example:

- It draws you closer to Allāh ﷻ.[246]
- It helps you keep your carnal desires under control.[247]

---

244 "Sex with your wives on the eve of fasting has been made permissible for you. They are clothing for you and you are clothing for them. Allāh knows that you were deceiving yourselves, so He accepted your repentance and forgave you. So now have relations with them and seek what Allāh has decreed for you. And eat and drink until the white thread becomes distinct from the black thread i.e. dawn, to you. Then complete the fast until nightfall [. . .]." (Sūrat al-Baqarah 187)

245 Ibn 'Umar ؓ related, "Allāh's Messenger ﷺ said, 'Islam is built on five [pillars]:

- To testify (*shahādah*) that there is no god except Allāh and Muḥammad is the messenger of Allāh
- To establish ritual prayer (*ṣalāh*)
- To purify [your] wealth (*zakāh*)
- To go for pilgrimage (*ḥajj*)
- And to fast (*ṣawm*) during *Ramaḍān*.'" (*Ṣaḥīḥ al-Bukhārī* 8)

246 Abū Hurayrah ؓ reported from the Prophet ﷺ, [who reported from Allāh ﷻ], "Every deed of Adam's descendant is for their personal benefit with the exception of *ṣawm*, for it is dedicated to me and I will compensate it." [The Prophet ﷺ continued], "The foul odour [which emanates from] a fasting person's mouth is more pleasant to Allāh than the fragrance of musk." (*Ṣaḥīḥ al-Bukhārī* 5928)

247 'Abdullāh [ibn Mas'ūd] ؓ reported, "We were [once] with the Prophet ﷺ and he suggested, 'Whoever can afford to get married should get married, for indeed marriage is the greatest source of lowering [one's] gaze [away from viewing illicit material] and is more protective of one's private parts [from engaging in impermissible

- It absolves you of sin.[248]
- It is a means of you being privileged to enter Paradise (*Jannah*) through an exclusive gate.[249]
- It will serve as a barrier for you against the Fire of Hell (*Jahannam*).[250]

WHO MUST FAST DURING RAMAḌĀN?

You must fast during *Ramaḍān*[251] if you are:

- Muslim.
- Mature (*bāligh*).[252]

---

sexual activities]. Whoever cannot afford to get married should fast, for indeed fasting will restrain their carnal desires for them.'" (*Ṣaḥīḥ al-Bukhārī* 1905)

248 Abū Hurayrah reported, "The Prophet said, '[. . .] whoever fasts during *Ramaḍān* with faith and anticipation of [Allāh's] reward will have their past sins forgiven for them.'" (*Ṣaḥīḥ al-Bukhārī* 1901)

249 Sahl reported, "The Prophet said, 'There is a gate in Paradise called *Rayyān* through which people who used to fast [frequently] will enter on the Day of Rising. No one will be able to enter through it apart from them. An announcement will be made, 'Where are those who used to fast [frequently]?' Hence they will rise [and enter the gate]. No one will enter through it except them. Once they have all entered [Paradise], the gate will be closed [forever]. No one will [be able to] enter through it [again].'" (*Ṣaḥīḥ al-Bukhārī* 1896)

250 Abū Hurayrah reported, "Allāh's Messenger said, 'Fasting is a shield [against the Fire of Hell] [. . .].'" (*Ṣaḥīḥ al-Bukhārī* 1894)

251 "You have believe, fasting is decreed for you just as it was decreed for those before you, so that you may become mindful [of Allāh]." (Sūrat al-Baqarah 183)

"[. . .] So whoever sights [the first moon of] the month, they must fast [for the entirety of that month]." (Sūrat al-Baqarah 185)

252 'Ā'ishah reported, "Allāh's Messenger said, 'The pen [used for documenting people's deeds] has been uplifted from [recording the actions of] three [types of people];

- A sleeping person, until they wake up

- Sane.[253]
- Free of slavery.
- Aware of the obligation of fasting.

CAN I BE EXCUSED FROM FASTING?

You do not have to fast during *Ramaḍān* if you are ill, or you are travelling to a destination that is beyond 77 km and you do not intend to stay at a particular location for more than 14 days at that destination. In these circumstances, you may forgo the fasts and make up for them at a later date.[254] If you are travelling, you should still try to fast, provided fasting will not have a negative impact on your health during your trip.

If you are pregnant or nursing a baby you will be excused from fasting during *Ramaḍān* if you fear that fasting will have a negative impact on your health or on your child's health. You will however have to make up for the missed fasts at a later date

If you are frail and do not possess the strength to fast or you are diagnosed with a chronic illness that prevents you from fasting,

---

- A child, until he becomes mature (*bāligh*)
- A [person who is] mentally challenged, until they begin to understand or regain their sanity.'" (*Sunan Ibn Mājah* 2041)

According to Sacred Law (*sharī'ah*) you become mature either by turning 15 years of age in lunar years, or;

- (Male): You have a wet dream before turning 15.
- (Female): You have your menses or a wet dream before turning 15.

253 ibid.

254 "So whoever among you is ill or on a journey—then an equal number of days [are to be fasted later to make up for the missed fasts]." (Sūrat al-Baqarah 184)

you are completely excused from fasting. You will instead give a payment (*fidyah*) of 1.6 kg of wheat or 3.2 kg of barley to a poor person or give its value in cash for each fast. No one can fast on your behalf.

Underage children should be encouraged to fast but not forced.

WHAT ARE THE PRECONDITIONS OF THE RAMAḌĀN FASTS?

- To make the intention to fast.[255]

  (1) If you were to abstain from eating, drinking and having sex throughout the day without making the intention to fast, you will not be considered a fasting person.

  (2) You are not required to verbally express your intention. Making an intention in your heart is sufficient.

  (3) You should make the intention to fast the night before. If however you fail to do so, you have up to midday to make it.

255 ʿUmar ibn al-Khaṭṭāb narrated, "I heard Allāh's Messenger say, 'Deeds are solely dependent on intentions, and every person will receive what they intended [. . .].'" (*Ṣaḥīḥ al-Bukhārī* 1)

- You must be free from menses (*ḥayḍ*) or postpartum bleeding (*nifās*).[256] Being pure from the state of major ritual impurity (*janābah*) is not a precondition for fasting.[257]
- You must be free from things that would nullify your fast.

WHAT ARE SOME RECOMMENDED ACTIVITIES FOR *ṢAWM*?

- To have the pre dawn meal (*suḥūr*).[258]
- To delay the pre dawn meal until shortly before dawn.[259]
- To hasten in breaking the fast immediately after sunset.
- To occupy your time in worship (*ʿibādah*).

---

256 Muʿādhah reported, "I asked ʿĀʾishah, 'What is the issue with women in their menses; they're supposed to make up the fasts [they missed during their period] but they're not supposed to make up for the prayers [they missed in that duration]?'

ʿĀʾishah asked, 'Are you a *Ḥarūrīyah* (i.e. from the *Khawārij* sect)?'

I replied, 'I am not a *Ḥarūrīyah*. I'm just asking.'

ʿĀʾishah explained, 'We used to experience this [during the Prophet's time] and we were simply instructed to make up for the [missed] fasts. We were not instructed to make up for the [missed] prayers.'" (*Ṣaḥīḥ Muslim* 763)

257 ʿĀʾishah and Umm Salamah both reported, "[At times] Allāh's Messenger would have *Fajr* come upon him while he was ritually impure (*janābah*) due to [having sexual relations] with his spouse. He would then bathe and fast." (*Ṣaḥīḥ al-Bukhārī* 1925)

258 Anas ibn Mālik reported, "Allāh's Messenger said, 'Have the pre dawn meal (*suḥūr*), for verily there are blessings in it." (*Ṣaḥīḥ Muslim* 2549)

259 Ibn ʿAbbās reported, "I heard Allāh's Messenger say, 'We, the fraternity of prophets, have been instructed to:

- Hasten in breaking our fast [immediately after sunset]
- Delay our pre dawn meal (*suḥūr*)
- Place our right hand over our left hand during the prayer.'" (*Majmaʿ al-Zawāʾid* 4880)

WHAT SHOULD I NOT DO WHEN FASTING?

- To chew on something.
- To taste something for no reason.
- To collect saliva in your mouth and then swallow it to quench your thirst.
- To engage in any type of sexual activity that would lead you to having sex. Minor acts of compassion are allowed though.[260]
- To engage in sinful acts such as backbiting, slandering and quarrelling.

WHAT INVALIDATES MY *ṢAWM* THUS RESULTING IN ME HAVING TO DO A MAKEUP (*QAḌĀ'*) *ṢAWM* AND GIVE A PENALTY (*KAFFĀRAH*)?

To deliberately break your *ṣawm* by eating, drinking or having sex, irrespective of whether you ejaculate or not, for no acceptable reason.[261]

---

260 'Ā'ishah ﷺ reported, "The Prophet ﷺ would kiss [his spouses] and have physical contact [with them] while fasting. He was more in control of his carnal desires than you." (*Ṣaḥīḥ al-Bukhārī* 1927)

261 Abū Hurayrah ﷺ reported, "[One day] while we were sitting with the Prophet ﷺ a man unexpectedly came and said, 'Messenger of Allāh, I have been ruined.'

Allāh's Messenger ﷺ asked, 'What happened to you?'

The man explained, 'I had sex with my wife while I was fasting.'

Allāh's Messenger ﷺ asked, 'Do you have a slave you can set free?'

He replied, 'No.'

The Messenger ﷺ asked, 'Can you fast for two months consecutively?'

- To swallow medication.
- To swallow the saliva of your spouse.

You will be excused from the *kaffārah* if you break your *ṣawm* due to becoming severely ill or after your menses (*ḥayḍ*) begins.

If you set out on a journey after deliberately breaking your *ṣawm*, you will not be excused from the *kaffārah*.

The *kaffārah* is;

- To fast for 60 consecutive days. If you are unable to do this, you may;
- Feed 60 people two meals.
- Feed one poor person two meals a day for 60 days.
- Give 60 poor people 1.6 kg of wheat or its equal value in cash.
- Give one poor person 1.6 kg of wheat or its equal value in cash every day for 60 consecutive days.

He replied, 'No.'

The Messenger ﷺ asked, 'Do you have the means to feed sixty impoverished people?'

He replied, 'No.'

The Prophet ﷺ then remained [silent]. While we were facing this situation somebody brought a basket of dates to the Prophet ﷺ. [. . .] The Prophet ﷺ asked, 'Where's the questioner?'

The man replied, 'Me [I'm here].'

The Prophet ﷺ instructed [him], 'Take this and donate it [to the poor].'

The man asked, '[Should I donate it] to someone poorer than me, Messenger of Allāh? I swear by Allāh, there is no family between Madīnah's two lava fields that is poorer than my family.'

The Prophet ﷺ then laughed to the extent that his premolars became visible. He then instructed, 'Feed it to your family.'" (*Ṣaḥīḥ al-Bukhārī* 1936)

Note: If while fasting for sixty consecutive days you decide to take a day off and not fast for any reason, with the exception of having your menses and postnatal bleeding, you will be required to restart your 60 days of fasting. All the fasts that were kept till that point will now be considered *nafl*.

WHAT INVALIDATES MY *ṢAWM* THUS RESULTING IN ME HAVING TO ONLY DO A MAKEUP (*QAḌĀʾ*) *ṢAWM*?

- To eat something that is not considered food e.g. paper, dough, flour etc.[262]
- To be forced to eat, drink or have sex.
- To take an enema or to insert medicinal drops into your nostrils.[263]
- To insert an object in your vagina e.g. tampon.
- To put eardrops in your ear.[264]
- To accidently swallow water when rinsing your mouth.
- To swallow blood mixed with your saliva when the taste of the blood is evident or the volume of blood is more than the saliva.
- To deliberately throw up a mouthful of vomit,[265] or to

262 Ibn ʿAbbās ﷺ said, "*Wuḍūʾ* simply becomes [required] due to things exiting the body, not by what enters it. A *ṣawm* is only broken by something that enters the body and not by what exits it." (*Sunan al-Kubrā al-Bayhaqī* 8253)

263 ibid.

264 ibid.

265 Abū Hurayrah ﷺ reported, "The Prophet ﷺ said, 'Whoever vomits while

unintentionally swallow vomit after vomiting, irrespective of its quantity.

- To eat or drink deliberately after eating or drinking accidently thinking that you broke your *ṣawm* by eating or drinking accidently.
- To have sex intentionally after having it accidently thinking that you broke your *ṣawm* by doing it accidently.
- To engage in other forms of sexual activity that result in ejaculation.
- To smoke.
- To inhale second hand smoke.
- To break the fast due to extreme hunger or thirst.
- To eat something stuck between your teeth that is the size of a chickpea or larger.
- To break your fast before sunset assuming the sun has already set.

WHAT ACTIVITIES WILL NOT INVALIDATE MY *ṢAWM* AT ALL?

- To eat, drink or have sex forgetfully.[266]

---

fasting, they are not obligated to make up that fast. If [however] they vomit deliberately, they must make up [that fast].'" (*Sunan Abū Dāwūd* 2380)

266 Abū Hurayrah ﷺ reported, "The Prophet ﷺ said, 'When [a person] forgets [that they're fasting] and then eats and drinks [something], they should complete their fast, for Allāh simply fed them and provided them with drink.'" (*Ṣaḥīḥ al-Bukhārī* 1933)

⬦ To have a wet dream.[267]

⬦ To kiss your spouse without swallowing their saliva.

⬦ To vomit unintentionally or to vomit less than a mouth full deliberately.[268]

⬦ To gather saliva in your mouth and swallow it.

⬦ To take an injection or give a blood test.

⬦ To apply *kohl* to your eyes.

⬦ To apply oil on to your body or hair.

⬦ To have water enter your ear holes while taking a bath or shower.

⬦ To clean your ears out with a cotton swab.

⬦ To swallow something stuck between your teeth that is smaller than a chickpea.

---

267 Abū Saʿīd al-Khudrī ⬥ reported, "The Prophet ⬥ said, 'There are three things that do not invalidate [the fast of] a fasting person; cupping, vomiting and having a wet dream.'" (*Jāmiʿ al-Tirmidhī* 719)

268 ibid.

Essential Traits

WHY AM I ALIVE?

Life is a gift from Allāh ﷻ. It is a blessing that has come with a purpose, a task and a goal. The purpose is that Allāh ﷻ examines your compliance to His orders[269], the task is to worship Him[270] and the goal is to earn His everlasting mercy and approval[271] thus making you eligible to be compensated with bliss both in this world and the next.[272]

In order to achieve the success of the two worlds you need to be acquainted with the tasks you have been assigned, the demeanour you must adopt and the culture you must embrace. Until then accomplishing Allāh's version of success is simply unrealistic. Hence the following is a collection of traits and tasks you are required to take on when working to this end.

Submission (Islām)

The first step you are required to take when striving to acquire Allāh's mercy is to submit to Allāh's authority in an uncompromised fashion. Allāh ﷻ has instructed, "You who believe, enter into submission completely [. . .]."[273] Essentially, you can only become genuinely obedient to Allāh ﷻ after you've taken this step. By submitting to Allāh ﷻ you will become praiseworthy in Allāh's eyes.

269 "[Allāh is the one] who created death and life in order to test you; which one of you is best in deeds. He is the Mighty, the Wise." (Sūrat al-Mulk 67:2)

270 "And I have created jinns and humans to simply worship me." (Sūrat al-Dhāriyāt 51:56)

271 "[. . .] and approval from Allāh is the greatest [acquisition]. That is the grand success." (Sūrat al-Tawbah 9:72)

272 "Whoever does a righteous deed regardless of whether they are male or female, as believers, We will definitely grant them a pleasant life. And We will certainly compensate them with their reward for the best of what they used to do." (Sūrat al-Naḥl 16:97)

273 Sūrat al-Baqarah 2:208

Abu Hurayrah ﷺ reported, "When [the verse], 'Everything that is in the heavens and earth belongs to Allāh. Whether you expose what is in [your heart] or conceal it, Allāh will hold you accountable for it [. . .],'[274] was revealed to Allāh's Messenger ﷺ, it was difficult for the companions of Allāh's Messenger ﷺ [to bear]. So they approached Allāh's Messenger ﷺ, knelt before him and expressed, 'Messenger of Allāh, we have been instructed to perform deeds we are capable of [doing]; praying, *jihād*, fasting and making charitable donations, however this verse has just been revealed to you which we are unable [to come to terms with].'

Allāh's Messenger ﷺ responded, 'Do you wish to say what the people of the two scriptures before you have said, 'We have heard and disobeyed?' Rather say, 'We have heard and obeyed and we seek your forgiveness, O our Sustainer, and to you is [our] place of return."

When people uttered these words and their tongues became submissive to it, Allāh immediately revealed, 'The Messenger has believed in what was revealed to him from his Sustainer, and [so have] the believers. All of them believe in Allāh, His angels, His books and His messengers, [saying], 'We make no distinction between any of His messengers.' And they say, 'We listen and we obey. [We seek] Your forgiveness, our Sustainer, and to You is [our final] destination."

When they did this Allāh abrogated [the previous verses] and revealed, 'Allāh compels a soul [to do] only [what is within] its capacity. The soul will bear [the results of] whatever [good] it has gained, and it will bear [the consequence of] whatever [evil] it has earned. [The people prayed] 'Our Master, do not impose blame on us if we have forgotten or erred.'

Allāh replied, 'Ok.'

---

274 Sūrat al-Baqarah 2:283

[They continued] 'Our Master, and do not impose a burden on us like You had imposed on those before us.'

He replied, 'Ok.'

[They asked] 'Our Master, and do not burden us with anything that we are unable to bear.'

He replied, 'Ok.'

[They concluded] 'And pardon us, forgive us, and have mercy on us. You are our Protector, so give us victory over the disbelieving people.' [275]

He replied, 'Ok.'" [276]

Repentance (Tawbah)

Upon completely submitting yourself to Allāh ﷻ you must immediately develop a healthy relationship with Him by repenting to Him over all your past misdeeds. Repentance entails:

- Regretting your misdeeds.
- Abandoning those misdeeds at once.
- Restoring the rights of those whose rights you have violated.
- Sincerely seeking Allāh's pardon and forgiveness.
- Making a commitment to Allāh ﷻ to never resort to those misdeeds again.

Repentance is something Allāh ﷻ has called His servants to.[277]

---

275 Sūrat al-Baqarah 2: 286

276 *Ṣaḥīḥ Muslim* 329

277 "You who believe, sincerely turn to Allāh in repentance. Your Sustainer will

There is no designated time for repenting[278] and there is no sin that is too great for Allāh ﷻ to forgive.[279] You can repent to Allāh ﷻ anytime for anything and *in-shā-Allāh* you will be forgiven. Allāh ﷻ becomes extremely delighted when His servant turns to Him for forgivness.[280]

---

erase your misdeeds [from your account] and will admit you into gardens beneath which rivers flow [. . .]."(Sūrat al-Taḥrīm 66:8)

278 Abū Mūsā al-Ash'arī ﷺ reported, "The Prophet ﷺ said, 'Allāh spreads His hand out during the night so that the sinner of the day may repent and He spreads out His hand during the day so that the sinner of the night may repent. [This will continue] until the sun will rise from its setting place (i.e. the west)." (*Ṣaḥīḥ Muslim* 6989)

279 Abū Sa'īd al-Khudrī ﷺ reported, "The Prophet ﷺ said, 'There was a man from the people before you who killed 99 people. He asked [people] about [who] the most knowledgeable person in the land [was] and was directed to a monk. He went to the monk and told him that he killed 99 people [and asked] if it was possible for him to repent. The monk replied, 'No.' So he killed the monk and completed 100 by murdering him.

He then asked [around] about [who] the most knowledgeable person in the land [was] and was directed to a scholar. [So he went to the scholar and] told him that he had killed 100 people; was it possible for him to repent?

The scholar answered, 'Yes. Who can stand between you and repentance? Go to such and such land, for there is a community there who worships Allāh the Exalted. You [also] worship [Allāh] with them. And do not return to your land for it is a land of evil.'

So he set out [to the recommended land] until, when he reached half way, death came to him. As a result the angels of mercy and the angels of punishment [came and] began arguing over him. The angels of mercy declared, 'He came in repentance with his heart turned to Allāh [so we will take him].'

The angels of punishment stated, 'He never did a good deed [in his entire life, therefore we will take him]!'

An angel then came [to them] in the form of a human, so the angels appointed him [to make a formal decision on this matter]. He suggested, 'Measure the distance between the two lands. Whichever one he is closer to, he will belong to it.'

So they measured the distance and found him to be closer to the land he intended [to go to]. Thus the angels of mercy took him.'" (*Ṣaḥīḥ Muslim* 7008)

280 Anas ﷺ reported, "Allāh's Messenger ﷺ said, 'Allāh becomes happier with the repentance of His servant, when the servant turns to Him [in repentance], than a person [who is faced with a situation where he is] on his riding camel in the desert

Our beloved Prophet ﷺ used to ask Allāh ﷻ for forgiveness every single day over what he perceived to be his shortcomings in executing his duties.[281] Thus repenting frequently is an emphasised *sunnah* of our beloved Prophet ﷺ.

Mindfulness of Allāh ﷻ (Taqwā)

The next step you need to take after settling your accounts with Allāh ﷻ and making the commitment to abstain from sin is to begin living a life of piety. Being habitually pious is only possible when you are constantly mindful of Allāh ﷻ. In reality your piety is proportionate to your consciousness of Allāh ﷻ. The greater your consciousness, the more motivated you will be to please Allāh ﷻ and the harder you will try to abstain from disobeying Allāh ﷻ.

Consciousness of Allāh ﷻ can be developed by:

⬦ Speaking about Allāh ﷻ frequently and remembering Him abundantly (*dhikr*).[282]

⬦ Asking Allāh ﷻ regularly to place a high level of His consciousness in your heart.[283]

---

and it [suddenly] escapes from him. The camel had his food and drinking [supplies tied] to it. He thus loses all hope [of surviving], approaches a tree and lies down in its shade [awaiting death]. He has lost all hope of [ever retrieving] his riding camel. While [he is] in this state the camel then suddenly comes and stands by him. So he takes it by its reins and says out of extreme joy, 'O Allāh, you are my servant and I am your Sustainer!'

He makes a mistake [in his statement] due to immense happiness.'" (*Ṣaḥīḥ Muslim* 6960)

281 Aghar ibn Yasār al-Muzanī ؓ reported, "Allāh's Messenger ﷺ said, "People! Turn to Allāh [in repentance] and seek his forgiveness, for indeed I turn [to Him in repentance] 100 times a day." (*Ṣaḥīḥ Muslim* 6859)

282 "And remind, for indeed the reminder benefits believers." (Sūrat al-Dhāriyāt 51:55)

"You who believe, remember Allāh frequently." (Sūrat al-Aḥzāb 33:41)

283 Ibn Masʿūd ؓ reported, "The Prophet ﷺ would often say, 'O Allāh, I ask

The more pious you become, the closer to Allāh ﷻ you will be[284] and the more successful you will become in the two worlds.[285]

The Prophetic Practice (Sunnah)

The life of piety has been thoroughly exemplified in the life and teachings of Allāh's Messenger, Muḥammad ﷺ.[286] True piety is to adopt the Messenger's ﷺ lifestyle without compromise.[287] By

---

you for guidance, piety (*tuqā*), chastity and independence." (*Ṣaḥīḥ Muslim* 6904)

284 Abū Hurayrah ؓ reported, "Some people asked [Allāh's Messenger ﷺ], 'Messenger of Allāh, who is the most noble person?'

He replied, 'The most pious of them.'

The questioners explained, 'We were not asking you about this.'

Allāh's Messenger ﷺ then said, "Then it is Yūsuf the Prophet of Allāh, who is the son of Allāh's Prophet, who is the son of Allāh's Prophet, who is the son of Allāh's best friend."

They said, 'We were not asking you about this either.'

Allāh's Messenger ﷺ asked, 'Are you asking me about the Arabs then? The best of them in the period of ignorance (*jāhilīyah*) is the best of them in Islam when they develop [an in-depth] comprehension (*fiqh*) [of the religion]'" (*Ṣaḥīḥ al-Bukhārī* 3353)

285 Abū Umāmah al-Bāhilī ؓ related, "I heard Allāh's Messenger ﷺ delivering a sermon during the 'Farewell Pilgrimage' saying, 'Be mindful of Allāh, your Sustainer, perform your five ritual prayers, fast during your month [of Ramaḍān], pay *zakāh* on your wealth and listen to your leaders, you will enter the paradise of your Sustainer [as a result]." (*Jāmiʿ al-Tirmidhī* 616)

286 "Certainly there lies an excellent example for you in the [life of] Allāh's Messenger; [an example] for those who anticipate [meeting] Allāh, [encountering] the final day and who remember Allāh frequently." (Sūrat al-Aḥzāb 33:21)

287 Ibn ʿAbbās ؓ reported, "The Prophet ﷺ stood among us to give a sermon and said, "You will be collected [on the Day of Judgement] in a manner that you will be barefooted, unclothed and uncircumcised; 'As We began the first creation, We will repeat it [. . .].' (Sūrat al-Anbiyāʾ 21:104)

The first of [Allāh's] creation to be clothed on the Day of Rising will be Ibrāhīm ؑ, the friend [of Allāh]. Men will be brought from my nation and will then be seized from [my] left [side]. I will say, 'O Sustainer, my Companions!'

Allāh will reply, 'You do not know what they introduced after you.'

I will then utter what the righteous slave [of Allāh i.e. ʿĪsā ؑ] will utter, 'And I was a witness over them [as long as I was among them; but when You had taken me,

adopting the Messenger's ﷺ example you will become Allāh's beloved,[288] earn eternal bliss[289] and be saved from deviating from the straight path.[290] You will become protected from everlasting torments in the hereafter.[291]

You were the Observer over them, and You are a Witness over all things. If You should punish them—indeed they are Your servants- but if You forgive them—indeed it is You who is the Exalted in Might,] the Wise.' (Sūrat al-Mā'idah 5:117–118)

[I will then] be told, "They continued to revert to their former ways [from the time you had left them]." (*Ṣaḥīḥ al-Bukhārī* 6526)

'Ābis ibn Rabī'ah ؓ reported, "'Umar ibn al-Khaṭṭāb ؓ went to the Black Stone, kissed it and said, 'I know that you are a stone that cannot harm [anyone] or benefit [anyone]. If I had not seen Allāh's Messenger ﷺ kiss you, I would not have kissed you.'" (*Ṣaḥīḥ al-Bukhārī* 1597)

288 "Say [Muḥammad ﷺ], 'If you love Allāh then follow me, Allāh will love you and forgive you of your sins.' Allāh is Ever Forgiving and Ever Merciful." (Sūrat Āle 'Imrān 3:31)

289 Abū Hurayrah ؓ reported, "Allāh's Messenger ﷺ said, 'Every [person from] my nation will enter paradise except for those who refuse to.'

The companions asked, 'Messenger of Allāh, who will refuse?'

He explained, 'Whoever obeys me will enter Paradise and whoever disobeys me has refused [to enter].'" (*Ṣaḥīḥ al-Bukhārī* 7280)

290 'Irbād ibn Sāriyah ؓ reported, "Allāh's Messenger ﷺ led us in prayer one day and then turned to us and gave us a profound speech through which [our] eyes shed tears and [our] hearts became frightened. One person expressed, 'Messenger of Allāh, this [speech] was as if it was the speech of a person bidding farewell. What are you entrusting us with?'

He replied, 'I am instructing you to be mindful of Allāh and to listen and obey [your leader] even [if he may be] an Abyssinian slave. Those from you who will continue to live after me will see great discord; hence [in such circumstances following] my traditions and the traditions of the honourable and guided successors will be obligatory for you. Cling to them and bite them with [your] molars. Beware of new matters [in the religion] for every new matter is an innovation (*bid'ah*) and every *bid'ah* is [an act of] misguidance.'" (*Sunan Abū Dāwūd* 4607)

291 Jābir ؓ reported, "Allāh's Messenger ﷺ said, 'My example and your example are of a man who lights a fire. [Suddenly] grasshoppers and moths begin falling into it while the man [tries to] drive them away. I am holding [you by] your belts away from the Fire [of Hell] but you are slipping away from my hand." (*Ṣaḥīḥ Muslim* 5958)

Numerous ways of performing good deeds

Identifying activities that are virtuous according to Allāh's standards is important for your spiritual progress.[292] No good deed is unworthy of carrying out regardless of how small it may seem.[293] You should constantly be looking for new ways within the *sunnah* framework to gain Allāh's proximity and you should always try to excel others.[294] You should understand that virtuous acts are not simply confined to various forms of ritual worship. Rather,

---

292 Abū Hurayrah ﷺ narrated, "The Prophet ﷺ said, "Faith (*īmān*) consists of over 60 branches; and modesty (*ḥayā'*) is a branch of *īmān*." (*Ṣaḥīḥ al-Bukhārī* 9)

Abū Dharr ﷺ reported, "Allāh's Messenger ﷺ said, 'Every morning a donation (*ṣadaqah*) is due for every healthy joint you have. Every *subḥān'Allāh* is a *ṣadaqah*. Every *alḥamdulillāh* is a *ṣadaqah*. Every *lā ilāha illallāh* is a *ṣadaqah*. Every *Allāhu akbar* is a *ṣadaqah*. Providing instructions to do the right thing is a *ṣadaqah*. Stopping [people] from wrongdoing is a *ṣadaqah*. Performing two units (*raka'āt*) [of *ṣalāh*] during the mid-morning will take care of all those donations.'" (*Ṣaḥīḥ Muslim* 1671)

Abū Dharr ﷺ reported, "The Prophet ﷺ said, 'The deeds of my nation were presented to me; both good and bad. I found removing harmful objects from the road to be among [people's] good deeds and I found sputum in the masjid which had not been buried [in the sand] to be among their bad deeds." (*Ṣaḥīḥ Muslim* 1233)

293 Abū Dharr ﷺ reported, "The Prophet ﷺ told me, 'Do not consider any good deed to be inferior, even if it may be meeting your brother with a cheerful face.'" (*Ṣaḥīḥ Muslim* 6690)

'Adī ibn Ḥātim ﷺ reported, "I heard the Prophet ﷺ say, 'Protect yourselves from the Fire [of Hell], even if [it may be by donating] a piece of a date.'" (*Ṣaḥīḥ al-Bukhārī* 1417)

294 Abū Dharr ﷺ reported, "Certain people from the Prophet's ﷺ companions said, 'Messenger of Allāh, the affluent people have taken off with the rewards [of the hereafter]. They pray as we pray, fast as we fast, and donate their surplus wealth.'

The Prophet ﷺ said, 'Has Allāh not made resources for you which you can donate? Every *subḥān'Allāh* is a *ṣadaqah*. Every *Allāhu akbar* is a *ṣadaqah*. Every *alḥamdulillāh* is a *ṣadaqah* and every *lā ilāha illallāh* is a *ṣadaqah*. Providing instructions to do good things is a *ṣadaqah* and stopping wrongdoing is a *ṣadaqah*. Having sex with your wives is a *ṣadaqah*.'

The companions asked, 'Messenger of Allāh, there is reward for us in fulfilling our carnal desires?'

He replied, 'What is your view if a person were to have unlawful sex; will there

working towards communal welfare and establishing social harmony is also a means of enhancing your spirituality.[295]

Hastening to do good deeds

Upon learning about a good deed or gaining the opportunity to perform one, you should avoid procrastinating in carrying it out.[296]

---

be sin upon him? Similarly when he has lawful sex he will be rewarded [for it].'" (*Ṣaḥīḥ Muslim* 2329)

Abū Hurayrah narrated, "Allāh's Messenger said, 'A *ṣadaqah* is due upon every healthy joint people have, every morning the sun rises. Establishing justice between two people is a *ṣadaqah*. Helping a man with his [riding] animal by helping him mount it is a *ṣadaqah*. Lifting his belongings onto it is a *ṣadaqah*. A good word is a *ṣadaqah*. Every step you take while walking to the [congregational] prayer is a *ṣadaqah*. Removing an obstacle from the road is a *ṣadaqah*." (*Ṣaḥīḥ Muslim* 2335)

295 Abū Hurayrah reported, "The Prophet said, 'I saw a man strolling in Paradise because he cut down a tree that was in the middle of the road. It was causing people inconvenience." (*Ṣaḥīḥ Muslim* 6671)

Abū Hurayrah reported, "Allāh's Messenger said, '[Once] while a man was walking along a road he became extremely thirsty. He found a well, climbed down into it and drank [some water]. He then came out and saw a dog panting and eating [wet] mud due to being thirsty. He said, 'This dog has reached the same level of thirst I had reached.'

So he climbed back down the well and filled his leather sock up with water. He then held the sock with his mouth until he climbed out [of the well] and gave the dog the water. Allāh expressed His gratitude over this to him and forgave him.'

The companions said, 'Messenger of Allāh, do we receive a reward for [serving] these types of animals?'

He replied, 'There is a reward for [serving] everything that possesses a moist liver [i.e. every living creature].'" (*Ṣaḥīḥ Muslim* 5859)

296 Abū Hurayrah reported, "Allāh's Messenger said, 'Hasten [to perform good] deeds [before the advent of] trials that will resemble the [progressive] portions of a dark night. A man will spend the morning a believer and become a disbeliever in the evening or a believer will spend the evening a believer and will become a disbeliever in the morning. He will sell his religion for the commodities of [this] world." (*Ṣaḥīḥ Muslim* 313)

Abū Hurayrah reported, "Allāh's Messenger said, 'Hasten [to perform good] deeds [before the emergence of] seven things. Are you simply waiting [to be

This was the practice of our beloved Prophet ﷺ.[297] Never be held back by unfavourable conditions, but rather take advantage of every second you get to progress in the line of spirituality.[298]

Reliance (Tawakkul)

When deciding to do a good deed it is important that you take up the means that are required to bring that deed into fruition. Upon adopting the required means you should execute the action to the best of your ability, and simultaneously rely on Allāh ﷻ for favourable results.[299] When you will rely on Allāh ﷻ in all your affairs Allāh ﷻ will love you,[300] take care of you[301] and provide

afflicted with] such poverty that will make [you] forget [about everything] or [to be privileged with] such affluence that will make [you] a transgressor or [to be diagnosed with] an illness that will spoil [your life] or [are you waiting for] old age that will make you senile or [for] a destructive death or [for] the 'Great Imposter' (*Dajjāl*) for [he is] an absent evil who is being awaited [for] or the 'Final Hour', for the 'Final Hour' is more afflicting and bitter." (*Jāmiʿ al-Tirmidhī* 2306)

297 'Uqbah ibn al-Ḥārith ؓ reported, 'I performed the *ʿAsr* prayer behind the Prophet ﷺ in Madīnah. He [concluded the prayer with] *salām* and got up quickly. He overstepped people's necks and [headed] to the home of one of his wives'. People were startled over his hastiness. He [later] came out to them and saw that they were startled over his impulsiveness so he explained, 'I recollected a piece of gold we had by us and I did not want it to hold me back so I ordered [my family] to give it [away to the poor]." (*Ṣaḥīḥ al-Bukhārī* 851)

298 Zubayr ibn 'Adī ؓ related, "We approached Anas ibn Mālik ؓ and complained to him about what people were experiencing with Ḥajjāj so he said, 'Be patient, for every era that will come upon you, the subsequent era will be worse than it. [This trend will continue] until you meet your Sustainer. I heard this from your Prophet ﷺ.'" (*Ṣaḥīḥ al-Bukhārī* 7068)

299 "[. . .] So when you have become determined, rely on Allāh [. . .]." (Sūrat Āle 'Imrān 3:159)

300 "[. . .] Surely, Allāh loves those who rely [on Him]." (Sūrat Āle 'Imrān 3:159)

301 'Umar ؓ reported, "Allāh's Messenger ﷺ said, 'If you were to rely on Allāh the way He deserves to be relied on, He would provide for you as He provides for

you hassle free access to Paradise (*Jannah*).³⁰² Ultimately you will become stress free in life.³⁰³

---

birds. They go out hungry in the morning and return satiated in the evening.'" (*Jāmiʿ al-Tirmidhī* 2344)

302 Ibn ʿAbbās ؓ related, "The Prophet ﷺ said [to a group of his companions], '[Many] nations were presented to me [in a dream]. As a result I saw a Prophet with a small group of people, and a Prophet with [only] one or two men, and a Prophet with no one [accompanying him] at all. Suddenly a great number of people were raised before me and I assumed that they were [all] my nation. I was told, 'This is Mūsā ؑ and his people. Instead, look at the horizon.' So I looked [at the horizon] and there was a great number of people [there]. I was then told, 'Look at the other horizon.' [I looked and again] there was a great number of people [there]. I was then informed, 'This is your nation. There will be seventy thousand people with them who will enter Paradise without any reckoning or [receiving any] punishment.'"

The Prophet ﷺ then got up [after relating this] and stepped into his house. People then began having a discussion over [who] those people [will be] who will enter Paradise without any reckoning or [receiving any] punishment. Some suggested, 'Maybe they will be those people who accompanied Allāh's Messenger ﷺ [during his prophethood].'

Others suggested, 'Maybe they will be those people who were born in Islam and did not associate anything with Allāh.' [Throughout the discussion] they suggested many things. Allāh's Messenger ﷺ then came out [of his house] to them and asked, 'What are you discussing?' They told him so he explained, 'They will be those who did not use charms or seek charms [from others] and they were not superstitious, rather they relied on their Sustainer.'" (*Ṣaḥīḥ Muslim* 527)

303 Jābir ibn ʿAbdullāh ؓ reported that he went on a journey with Allāh's Messenger ﷺ to Najd. When Allāh's Messenger ﷺ returned, he returned with him. They were caught up by midday in a valley that had many thorn-trees. Allāh's Messenger ﷺ settled down and people dispersed seeking the shade of the trees [in the valley]. Allāh's Messenger ﷺ lodged under a tree and hung his sword on it. We went to sleep for a while when suddenly Allāh's Messenger ﷺ summoned us. There was a Bedouin by him. The Prophet ﷺ explained, 'This individual unsheathed my sword over me while I was sleeping. I woke up and [saw the] sword in his hand unsheathed. He [then] asked, 'Who will protect you from me?'

I replied three times, 'Allāh."

The Messenger ﷺ did not punish him [. . .]." (*Ṣaḥīḥ al-Bukhārī* 2910)

Sincerity (Ikhlāṣ)

While working diligently to earn Allāh's approval and mercy you need to ensure that every good deed you carry out is solely dedicated to Allāh ﷻ. A good deed is as good as its intention in Allāh's court.[304] Hence if a good deed is dedicated to Him, it will be rewarded and will serve as a means of gaining His proximity. If however it is not dedicated to Him but rather done with other motives in mind, it will have no merit in Allāh's eyes.[305] Instead, it will be a means of you becoming more distant from Allāh ﷻ irrespective of how pious you may appear to be in society.[306]

Moderation

If you wish to add voluntary (*nafl*) activities into your daily routine, you must ensure that you practice them with moderation.[307] You must avoid becoming occupied in these activities in a manner that

---

304 ʿUmar ibn al-Khaṭṭāb ؓ narrated, "I heard Allāh's Messenger ﷺ say, 'Deeds are solely dependent on intentions, and every person will receive what they intended.'" (*Ṣaḥīḥ al-Bukhārī* 1)

305 Abū Mūsā al-Ashʿarī ؓ reported, "Allāh's Messenger ﷺ was asked about:

- a man who fights [in a battle] out of bravery
- [a man who] fights out of fanaticism and
- [a man who] fights to show off;

which one of them is considered to be in Allāh's path? Allāh's Messenger ﷺ replied, 'Whoever fights so that Allāh's word becomes elevated, he is in Allāh's path.'" (*Ṣaḥīḥ Muslim* 4920)

306 Abū Hurayrah ؓ reported, "Allāh's Messenger ﷺ said, 'Allāh does not look at your appearances nor at your wealth, rather he looks at your hearts and deeds.'" (*Ṣaḥīḥ Muslim* 6543)

307 Abū Hurayrah ؓ narrated, "The Prophet ﷺ said, 'Indeed, the religion (*dīn*) is easy. And whoever adopts rigidity in the *dīn*, it will overwhelm them. So be balanced and moderate, and rejoice. Seek [Allāh's] assistance [by worshipping Him for a short period] in the morning and in the evening and for a short while during the final hours of the night.'" (*Ṣaḥīḥ al-Bukhārī* 39)

it compromises your other duties and responsibilities.[308] Being inflexible in this area will only yield adverse results.[309] You must

308 Anas ibn Mālik ◈ reported, "A group of three people went to the homes of the wives of the Prophet ◈ to ask [them] about the rituals the Prophet ◈ [performed while at home]. When the group was told [about his practices], it seemed as if they found it to be less [than what they had expected]. They then expressed, 'Where are we in connection with the Prophet ◈? Allāh has forgiven him of his past and future misdeeds.'

One of them vowed, 'As for me, I will [begin to] pray all night forever.'

The other said, 'I will [start] fasting throughout time and will never give up.'

The other person said, 'I will stay away from women and will never get married.'

Allāh's Messenger ◈ [later] went to them and asked, 'Are you the ones who said such and such? By Allāh, I am more fearful of Allāh and more mindful of Him than [all of] you, however, I fast and skip fasts, I pray and I sleep [throughout the night] and I marry women. Whoever disregards my traditions (sunnah) has no connection with me.'" (*Ṣaḥīḥ al-Bukhārī* 5063)

Anas ibn Mālik ◈ reported, "The Prophet ◈ entered [the masjid] and noticed a rope that was [tied] stretching between two pillars. He asked, 'What is this rope [here for]?'

The companions explained, 'This is Zaynab's rope. When she becomes tired [while praying] she hangs [on to it to help her carry on].'"

The Prophet ◈ demanded, "No, untie it. You should pray while you are fresh. When [you] become tired [you] should take a seat [and rest]." (*Ṣaḥīḥ al-Bukhārī* 1150)

309 'Abdullāh [ibn Mas'ūd] ◈ reported, "Allāh's Messenger ◈ said, 'The inflexible people have perished.' He repeated these words three times." (*Ṣaḥīḥ Muslim* 6784)

'Abdullāh ibn 'Amr ibn al-'Āṣ ◈ related, "Allāh's Messenger ◈ asked me, "Abdullāh, have I not been informed that you fast all day and stand [in prayer] all night [every single day]?'

I replied, 'Yes Messenger of Allāh, [that is true].'

He said, 'Do not do [as such]. Fast [some days] and skip fasting [on other days]. Stand [in prayer for a portion of the night] and go to sleep [in the other portion], for indeed your body has a right over you, your eyes have a right over you, your wife has a right over you, your visitors have a right over you. Fasting for three days every month is enough for you. You will receive ten times the equivalent [reward] for every single good deed [you do]. Thus, this will [translate for you as] fasting for the entire year.'

[Unfortunately] I became stringent. As a result, strictness was exercised with me. I said, 'Messenger of Allāh, I find strength [in me to do more].'

He replied, 'Then keep the fast of Allāh's Prophet, Dāwūd ◈, and do not [attempt] to do more.'

realize that the sole objective of performing *nafl* deeds is to earn Allāh's approval and mercy; not to make a statement to the community or to try and experience a spiritual trance.[310]

Steadfastness (Istiqāmah)

Consistency in your daily practices is also essential for your spiritual development. This is what was instructed and practiced by our beloved Messenger ﷺ.[311]

I asked, 'What are the fasts of Allāh's Prophet Dāwūd ﷺ?'

He answered, 'Half the year.'

After reaching old age 'Abdullāh would say, 'How I wish I had accepted the leniency [offered by] the Prophet ﷺ.'" (*Ṣaḥīḥ al-Bukhārī* 1975)

310 Ḥanẓalah al-Usayyidī ﷺ related, "Abū Bakr ﷺ met me [one day] and asked, 'How are you Ḥanẓalah?'

I replied, 'Ḥanẓalah has become a hypocrite.'

Abū Bakr ﷺ expressed, '*SubḥānAllāh*, what are you saying?'

I explained, 'We are normally with Allāh's Messenger ﷺ who reminds us of the Fire [of Hell] and Paradise as if it is before our very eyes. When we leave the company of Allāh's Messenger ﷺ we tend to our wives, children and property and forget many things.'

Abū Bakr ﷺ said, 'By Allāh, we are experiencing something similar to this.'

Hence, Abū Bakr ﷺ and I went and visited Allāh's Messenger ﷺ. I then expressed, 'Ḥanẓalah has become a hypocrite, Messenger of Allāh.'

Allāh's Messenger ﷺ asked, 'How so?'

I explained, 'Messenger of Allāh, we are normally with you as you remind us of the Fire [of Hell] and Paradise as if it is before our very eyes. When we leave your company we tend to our wives, children and property and forget many things.'

Allāh's Messenger ﷺ said, 'I swear by He in whose hands my life is, if you were to always remain in the condition you're in when being with me and during the [sessions of] remembrance, the angels would shake your hand in your bed and on your pathway, however Ḥanẓalah there is time for this and a time for that.'" (*Ṣaḥīḥ Muslim* 6966)

311 Sufyān ibn 'Abdullāh ﷺ related, "I requested, 'Messenger of Allāh, tell me something about Islam which I will not have to ask anyone about besides you.'

He said, 'Say, 'I believe in Allāh,' and then remain steadfast.'" (*Ṣaḥīḥ Muslim* 159)

Prayer (Duʿāʾ)

Another essential ingredient for developing a healthy relationship with Allāh ﷻ is to pray to Him regularly.[312] Allāh ﷻ has instructed us all to ask favours from Him through *duʿāʾ*.[313] *Duʿāʾ* is considered to be the essence of ritual worship,[314] for it is an expression of the utmost humility in front of Allāh ﷻ. You should develop the habit to ask Allāh ﷻ for anything you need,[315] for no *duʿāʾ* ever goes in vain.[316]

The proper etiquette for making a *duʿāʾ* is:

---

312 "And when My servants ask you about Me, so indeed I am near. I respond to the call of the caller when they call upon Me. Hence they should respond to My call and believe in Me so that they may be guided." (Sūrat al-Baqarah 2:186)

313 "And your Sustainer says, 'Call upon Me, I will respond to you. Surely those who are [too] arrogant to worship Me will soon enter Hell in a disgraced fashion." (Sūrat al-Ghāfir 40:60)

314 Anas ibn Mālik ؓ reported, "The Prophet ﷺ said, '*Duʿāʾ* is the brain of ritual worship.'" (*Jāmiʿ al-Tirmidhī* 3371)

315 Ibn ʿUmar ؓ said, "I make a *duʿāʾ* for every issue of mine. [I even pray that] Allāh expands the strides of my riding animal. [I continue doing this] until I witness what pleases me regarding that [prayer]." (*Adab al-Mufrad* 617)

Abū Hurayrah ؓ reported, "The Prophet ﷺ said, 'Whoever does not ask Allāh [for whatever they need], Allāh becomes displeased with them.'" (*Adab al-Mufrad* 658)

316 Abū Hurayrah ؓ reported, "Allāh's Messenger ﷺ, 'Your *duʿāʾ* will be accepted as long as you are not impatient, [by] saying, 'I prayed but I did not get any response."" (*Adab al-Mufrad* 655)

Abū Saʿīd al-Khudrī ؓ reported, "The Prophet ﷺ said, 'Every Muslim who makes a *duʿāʾ* which does not consist of a [request for] sin or the severance of ties will be granted one of three things:

- Either their *duʿāʾ* is answered immediately
- Or [Allāh] stores the *duʿāʾ* for them in the hereafter [as a reward]
- Or [Allāh] removes an adversity that is proportionate to [the sincerity of their *duʿāʾ*].'

Someone remarked, 'In that case [people's] *duʿāʾ* will increase.'

The Prophet ﷺ said, 'Allāh is greater in terms of increasing [his acceptance of people's *duʿāʾ*].'" (*Adab al-Mufrad* 710)

- Adopt a posture that displays humility.
- Cup your palms in front of your face.[317]
- Praise Allāh ﷻ.[318]
- Pray for the Prophet ﷺ.[319]
- Ask Allāh ﷻ to forgive you of your past misdeeds.
- Ask Allāh ﷻ sincerely for whatever you require.[320]
- Have full confidence that your request will be honoured and accepted.[321]

---

317 ʿUmar ibn al-Khaṭṭāb related, "Whenever Allāh's Messenger ﷺ raised his hands for *duʿā'*, he would not put them down until he wiped his face with them." (*Jāmiʿ al-Tirmidhī* 3386)

Wahb reported, "I saw Ibn ʿUmar and Ibn al-Zubayr making a *duʿā'*. They cupped their palms in front of their faces." (*Adab al-Mufrad* 609)

318 Faḍālah ibn ʿUbayd reported, "Allāh's Messenger ﷺ heard a man pray during *ṣalāh*. He neither glorified Allāh nor did he pray for the Prophet ﷺ. So Allāh's Messenger ﷺ expressed, 'This person was hasty.' He then called him and either said to him or to someone else, 'When any of you pray, you should begin by glorifying your Master and praising Him, and then pray for the Prophet ﷺ. After that, you should ask for whatever you like.'" (*Sunan Abū Dāwūd* 1481)

319 ibid.

320 ʿAbd al-Raḥmān ibn Yazīd related, "Rabīʿ used to visit ʿAlqamah every Friday. When I would not be there they would send for me. Once Rabīʿ came by when I was not there. [Later] ʿAlqamah met me and told me, 'Have you not seen what [comments] Rabīʿ has brought forth? He said, 'Do you not see how frequently people pray and how seldom their [call] is answered? That is because Allāh accepts only sincere prayers."

I asked, 'Didn't ʿAbdullāh [ibn Masʿūd] say [something like that]?'

He asked, 'What did he say?'

I said, "Abdullāh said, 'Allāh does not listen to someone who wants others to hear [their prayer], or to a show-off, or to a person playing around. [He only listens] to a person who prays firmly [and sincerely] from their heart."" (*Adab al-Mufrad* 606)

321 Anas reported, "Allāh's Messenger ﷺ said, 'When you pray, put your

◇ Do not ask for negative things.[322]

Social Conduct

While working on your relationship with Allāh ﷻ you must also work on being a dignified person in society. This can be accomplished by adopting the noble behaviour and qualities of our beloved Messenger ﷺ.[323] You must realize that being well behaved in the community is also a means of gaining Allāh's proximity[324] and achieving optimum results in the Hereafter.[325] Being rude and

---

heart in [your] prayer. Do not say, 'O Allāh if you wish then grant me,' for there is nothing that can force Allāh [against His will].'" (*Adab al-Mufrad* 608)

Abū Hurayrah ؓ reported, "Allāh's Messenger ﷺ said, 'When you make a prayer, do not say, 'If you wish [O Allāh]. . .' Ask with confidence. Increase [your] inclination [to the Almighty], for indeed nothing is difficult for Allāh to grant.'" (*Adab al-Mufrad* 607)

322 Abū Hurayrah ؓ reported, "Ṭufayl ibn ʿAmr al-Dawsī came to Allāh's Messenger ﷺ and said, 'Messenger of Allāh, [the people of] Daws have disobeyed [me] and have refused [to accept Islam] so ask Allāh to curse them.'

Allāh's Messenger ﷺ then turned to the *qiblah* and raised his hands. People assumed that he was going to curse them. He prayed, 'O Allāh, guide [the people of] Daws and bring them [to the straight path].'" (*Adab al-Mufrad* 611)

323 ʿAbdullāh ibn ʿAmr ؓ reported, "The Prophet ﷺ was neither obscene [by nature] nor did he act obscene. He would [often] say, 'The best of you is the one who has the best behaviour among you.'" (*Adab al-Mufrad* 271)

Jarīr ؓ related, "Ever since I embraced Islam the Messenger ﷺ has always looked at my face with a smile." (*Adab al-Mufrad* 250)

324 ʿAbdullāh ibn ʿAmr ؓ reported, "Allāh's Messenger ﷺ used to often pray, 'O Allāh, I ask You for health, restraint, trustworthiness, good character and contentment with the decree.'" (*Adab al-Mufrad* 307)

325 Abū Dardā' ؓ reported, "The Prophet ﷺ said, 'Nothing will be heavier on the scale [of deeds on the Day of Judgement] than good character.'" (*Adab al-Mufrad* 270)

ʿAmr ibn Shuʿayb reported from his father, who reported from ʿAmr's grandfather ؓ who heard the Prophet ﷺ say, 'Should I tell you who the most beloved person is to me from among you and who will be sitting the closest to me on the Day of Rising?'

The companions (*ṣaḥābah*) remained silent, so the Messenger ﷺ repeated his question two to three times again. The companions then replied, 'Yes, Messenger of Allāh.'

arrogant on the other hand will make you worthless in the eyes of the Almighty[326] irrespective of how knowledgeable you are or how great of a worshipper you may be.

He said, 'The one who has the best behaviour from you.'" (*Adab al-Mufrad* 272)

326 'Abdullāh ibn 'Amr ﷺ related, "We were sitting with Allāh's Messenger ﷺ when a Bedouin wearing a robe approached the Messenger ﷺ and stood before him. He said [to the *ṣaḥābah*], 'Your companion [here i.e. the Prophet ﷺ] has disgraced every horseman—or he said—He intends to disgrace every horseman—and elevate every shepherd.' The Prophet ﷺ took hold of the folds of his robe and said, 'Do I not see the garments of the imbecilic on you?'

Thereafter the Prophet ﷺ explained, 'When Allāh's Prophet, Nūḥ ﷺ was approached by death, he said to his son, 'I am going to give you some instructions. I instruct you to do two things and forbid you from two things. I order you [to say],

- 'There is no god except Allāh (*Lā ilāha illallāh*).' If the seven heavens and the seven earths were to be put on a pan [of a scale] and [the phrase] '*Lā ilāha illallāh*' was put in the [other] pan, the pan with *Lā ilāha illallāh* would outweigh [the other pan]. If the seven heavens and the seven earths were an obscure ring, [the phrase] '*Lā ilāha illallāh*' would break it.
- '*SubḥānAllāhi wa bi ḥamdihi*.' This is a prayer for every [situation] and it is through this that everything is granted provisions.

And I forbid you to associate others (*shirk*) with Allāh [in His divinity] and to be arrogant.'

So I asked—or someone else asked, 'Messenger of Allāh, we are acquainted with this *shirk* [concept, however] what is arrogance? Is it a garment of ours which we wear?'

The Prophet ﷺ replied, 'No.'

The person asked, 'Is it a pair of attractive footwear of ours with nice laces?'

The Prophet ﷺ replied, 'No.'

The person asked, 'Is it a riding animal of ours which we mount?'

The Prophet ﷺ replied, 'No.'

The person asked, 'Is it a group of our companions who sit with us?'

The Prophet ﷺ replied, 'No.'

The person asked, 'Messenger of Allāh, what is arrogance then?'

The Prophet ﷺ explained, 'To repel the truth and to consider people [to be] inferior.'" (*Adab al-Mufrad* 548)

Abū Hurayrah ﷺ reported, "The Prophet ﷺ said, 'Allāh the Almighty said, 'Might is My wrapper (*izār*) and pride is My cloak. Whoever contends with Me over any one of them, I will punish them.''" (*Adab al-Mufrad* 552)

'Abdullāh ibn 'Amr ﷺ related, "The Prophet ﷺ said, 'The arrogant people will

Conduct with Your Parents

The people you need to care about the most are your parents.[327] Amongst your parents, your mother deserves greater attention than your father.[328] Making them happy is to make Allāh 🕮 happy and making them upset is to make Allāh 🕮 displeased.[329] You should overlook the improper treatment you may sometimes receive from them.[330]

---

be collected like ants in the form of men on the Day of Rising. They will be draped in shame from every corner. They will be driven to a prison in Hell called Bōlas. The fire of fires will rise over them. They will be given the foul pus of the dwellers of Hell as drink.'" (*Adab al-Mufrad* 557)

327 "And we have instructed man to [adopt] goodness with his parents [. . .]" (Sūrat al-'Ankabūt 29: 8)

328 Bahz ibn Ḥakīm reported from his father, who reported from his grandfather 🕮 who related, "I asked [the Prophet 🕮], 'Messenger of Allāh, who should I listen to?'
'Your mother,' he replied.
I asked, '[Then] who should I listen to?'
'Your mother,' he replied.
I asked, '[Then] who should I listen to?'
'Your mother,' he replied.
I asked, '[Then] who should I listen to?'
'Your father,' he replied, 'And then the next closest relative and then the next.'" (*Adab al-Mufrad* 3)

329 'Abdullāh ibn 'Umar 🕮 reported, "The Sustainer's happiness lies in the happiness of [your] parent, and the Sustainer's anger lies in the anger of [your] parent." (*Adab al-Mufrad* 2)

Mu'ādh 🕮 said, "The Prophet 🕮 said, 'May happiness be for the person who listens to their parents. May Allāh the Almighty prolong their life.'" (*Adab al-Mufrad* 22)

330 Ibn 'Abbās 🕮 related, "Allāh opens two gates [of Paradise] for every Muslim who has two Muslim parents whom he serves [after waking up] in the morning and anticipates [Allāh's reward for his services]. If they have only one parent, then [Allāh will open up only] one [gate for them]. If they displease any one of them Allāh will remain displeased with them until the parent becomes pleased with them."

Someone asked, "Even if they did not treat them well?"

"Even if they did not treat them well," he replied. (*Adab al-Mufrad* 7)

You should go out of your way to help them,[331] to listen to them[332]

---

331 Sa'īd ibn Abū Burdah reported, "I heard my father relate, 'Ibn 'Umar ﷺ saw a Yamānī man performing *ṭawāf* of the [Ka'bah] while carrying his mother on his back, saying;

'I am her humble camel

If her mount is frightened, I am not frightened.'

He then asked, 'Ibn 'Umar, do you think I have repaid her [for the favours she's done for me throughout my life]?'

He replied, 'No, [you haven't even repaid her] for a single groan [she made during her labour].'" (*Adab al-Mufrad* 11)

332 Abū Hurayrah ﷺ reported, "I heard Allāh's Messenger ﷺ relate, 'No human child has ever spoken in the cradle except for 'Īsā ibn Maryam ﷺ and the child associated with Jurayj.'

Someone asked, 'Prophet of Allāh, who was the child associated with Jurayj?'

The Prophet ﷺ replied, 'Jurayj was a monk who lived in a hermitage of his. There was a cowherd who used to take shelter at the base of his hermitage and a woman from the village used to interact with him [regularly]. One day Jurayj's mother came while he was praying and called out, 'Jurayj!'

He said to himself while praying, '[Should I tend to] my mother or [continue with] my prayer?'

He decided to give preference to his prayer. She then called out to him for a second time and he again asked himself, '[Should I tend to] my mother or [continue with] my prayer?'

He felt that he should give preference to his prayer [and continued]. She then called out to him for a third time and yet again he asked himself, '[Should I tend to] my mother or [continue with] my prayer?'

He again concluded that he should give preference to his prayer. When he ended up not answering her, she said, 'Jurayj, may Allāh not let you experience death until you have looked at the faces of shameless women,' and left.

The village woman was [later] brought before the king after having given birth to a child. He asked, 'Whose [child] is it?'

She replied, 'Jurayj's.'

He asked, 'The man in the hermitage?!'

'Yes,' she answered.

He ordered [his men], 'Destroy his hermitage and bring him to me.'

The men went and hacked at his hermitage with axes until it collapsed. They then tied his hands to his neck with a rope and took him to the king. [On the way] he passed by some shameless women. He looked at them and smiled. They also looked at him along with the public [gathered there]. The king asked, 'What does this woman claim?'

and to please them[333] every single day. Be extremely cautious of mistreating them as this will only lead to grave consequences both in this world and the next.[334]

He asked, 'What does she claim?'

He replied, 'She claims that her child is from you.'

He asked her, 'You're making this claim?'

She replied, 'Yes.'

He asked, 'Where is the little one?'

The people replied, 'He is there in her room.'

He then went to the child and asked it, 'Who is your father?'

The child replied, 'The cowherd,'

The king then proposed [remorsefully], 'Shall we [re]construct your hermitage out of gold?'

He replied, 'No.'

The king asked, 'Out of silver?'

'No,' he replied.

The king asked, 'How shall we make it [then]?'

He said, 'Restore it the way it was.'

The king then asked, 'What made you smile?'

'Something I realized. My mother's prayer had overtaken me.'

He then related [the incident] to them.'" (*Adab al-Mufrad* 33)

333 Abū Murrah ﷺ reported, "Marwān used to make Abū Hurayrah ﷺ his deputy [governor of Madīnah when going on a trip]. Abū Hurayrah used to reside in Dhū al-Ḥulayfah. His mother stayed in one house while he stayed in another. When he wanted to go out, he would stop at her door and say, 'Peace be upon you, Mother, along with Allah's mercy and blessings.'

She would reply, 'And peace be upon you, my beloved son, along with Allah's mercy and blessings.'

Then he would say, 'May Allah have mercy on you [just as you had mercy on me] when you raised me as a child.'

She would answer, 'May Allah have mercy on you as you have been respectful to me in my old age.'

After that if he wanted to go inside, he would do the same thing." (*Adab al-Mufrad* 12)

334 Abū Bakrah ﷺ reported, "Allāh's Messenger ﷺ [once] asked a few times, 'Should I not tell you of the greatest sins?' The companions replied 'Yes, Messenger of Allāh.' He said, 'Performing *shirk* with Allāh and disobeying [your] parents.' He

Conduct with Your Spouse

Healthy families build healthy communities and healthy communities build healthy societies. Healthy families are simply developed through healthy marital relations. The only time a married couple can genuinely have a healthy relationship is when they truly have compassion for one another and are appreciative of each other.[335]

Couples should avoid pursuing each other's faults and should focus on helping each other become better people.[336]

---

then sat up after reclining and said, 'And false testimonies.' He continued to repeat this until I said [to myself], 'I wish he would become silent.'" (*Adab al-Mufrad* 15)

Abū Hurayrah ✿ reported, "The Prophet ✿ said, 'May that person be disgraced! May that person be disgraced! May that person be disgraced!' The companions asked, 'Who, Messenger of Allāh?' He said, 'The person who finds [both of] their parents with them in old age, or one of them, and enters the Fire [of Hell for failing to serve them].'" (*Adab al-Mufrad* 21)

Abū Ṭufayl ✿ reported, "Someone asked ʿAlī ✿ 'Did the Prophet ✿ ever share anything with you which he did not share with anyone else?' He replied, 'Allāh's Messenger ✿ did not share anything with me which he did not share with the rest of the people except for what I have in my sword's cover.'

He then took out a document. In it was written, 'May Allāh curse the person who slaughters an animal on the name of something besides Allāh. May Allāh curse the person who steals the boundary markers of the land. May Allāh curse the person who curses their parents. May Allāh curse the person who provides shelter to a [religious] innovator (*muḥdith*)." (*Adab al-Mufrad* 17)

ʿAbdullāh ibn ʿAmr ✿ said, "The Prophet ✿ said, 'One enormity is that a person swears at their parents.'

The companions asked, 'How could they swear at them?' He explained, 'They swear at a man who in turn swears at their father and mother.' (*Adab al-Mufrad* 27)

335   "[. . .] and live with them in kindness [. . .]." (Sūrat al-Nisāʾ 4:19)

Abū Hurayrah ✿ reported, "Allāh's Messenger ✿ said, 'The most perfect of believers in [their] belief are [those who are] the best of them in character. The best of you are those who are the best [behaved] with their women." (*Jāmiʿ al-Tirmidhī* 1162)

336   "[. . .] and if you dislike them then perhaps you may dislike something while Allāh has placed great good in it." (Sūrat al-Nisāʾ 4:19)

Abū Hurayrah ✿ reported, "Allāh's Messenger ✿ said, 'A male believer should not hate a female believer. If he dislikes something of her character, he will be pleased with another trait of hers.'" (*Ṣaḥīḥ Muslim* 3645)

As a husband you must take care of your wife's essential needs such as clothing, food and shelter, and you must completely avoid being abusive to her.[337] You must understand that spending on your family is one of the best forms of charity (*ṣadaqah*).[338] Compromising your duties to your family will simply make you distant from Allāh ﷻ.[339]

As a wife you should be prompt in fulfilling your husband's carnal desires.[340] In his absence you must protect your chastity

---

337 Muʿāwiyah al-Qushayrī ؓ related, "I asked [the Messenger ﷺ], 'Messenger of Allāh, what are the rights of our wives over us?' He explained, 'You feed her when you eat and clothe her when you clothe yourself. Do not strike her face nor slander her, and do not leave her [alone] except in the house.'" (*Sunan Abū Dāwūd* 2142)

338 Abū Hurayrah ؓ reported, "Allāh's Messenger ﷺ said, 'There is a dinar that you spend in Allāh's path, a dinar that you spend on freeing a slave, a dinar that you donate to someone in need and a dinar that you spend on your family. The [dinar that brings about] the greatest reward [from Allāh] is the one you spend on your family.'" (*Ṣaḥīḥ Muslim* 2311)

Abū Masʿūd al-Badrī ؓ reported, "The Prophet ﷺ said, 'When a man spends on his family, anticipating reward [from Allāh] for it, the spending is [treated as] a donation (*ṣadaqah*) for him.'" (*Ṣaḥīḥ al-Bukhārī* 55)

339 ʿAbdullāh ibn ʿAmr ibn ʿĀs ؓ related, "Allāh's Messenger ﷺ said, 'It is sufficient for a man to be rendered a sinner by his withholding [the provisions] of those whose provisions he [is responsible for].'" (*Ṣaḥīḥ Muslim* 2312)

340 Ṭalq ibn ʿAlī ؓ reported, "Allāh's Messenger ﷺ said, 'When a man calls his wife for his [sexual] needs, she should go to him even if she is [cooking] by the oven.'" (*Jāmiʿ al-Tirmidhī* 1160)

Abū Hurayrah ؓ reported, "Allāh's Messenger ﷺ said, 'When a man calls his wife to bed and she refuses [to go to him without a reasonable excuse], as a result he spends the night upset with her, the angels curse her until she wakes up in the morning.'" (*Ṣaḥīḥ al-Bukhārī* 3237)

Umm Salamah ؓ reported, "Allāh's Messenger ﷺ said, 'Whichever woman dies while her husband is pleased with her will enter Paradise.'" (*Jāmiʿ al-Tirmidhī* 1161)

along with the house and the household belongings.[341] No one should ever enter your home without your husband's permission.[342]

Conduct with Your Children

Children are one of Allāh's greatest blessings. They are our future and our support at the time of need. As a parent, you have the responsibility of providing them with the best upbringing they can ever have,[343] and to show them unconditional love.[344] You must avoid any preferential treatment between them and be absolutely fair with them at all times.[345]

---

341 Ibn ʿUmar ﵁ reported, "I heard Allah's Messenger ﷺ say, 'All of you are shepherds and each one of you will be questioned about their flock. [. . .] A woman is a shepherd in her husband's house and she will be questioned about her flock [. . .].'" (*Ṣaḥīḥ al-Bukhārī* 893)

342 Abū Hurayrah ﵁ reported, "Allāh's Messenger ﷺ said, 'A woman is not allowed to fast [voluntarily] while her husband is present [at home], except if he allows [her]. [In his absence] she must not allow anyone in his house except with his permission. Whatever she spends [from his earnings that exceed her needs] without his permission, he will have his share returned to him.'" (*Ṣaḥīḥ al-Bukhārī* 5195)

343 Numayr ibn Aws ﵁ said, "The [Prophet's companions] would often say, 'Piety is from Allāh while discipline is from the parents.'" (*Adab al-Mufrad* 92)

344 ʿĀʾishah ﵂ said, "A group of Bedouins [once] came to the Prophet ﷺ. One of their men asked, 'Messenger of Allāh, do you [actually] kiss children? By Allāh, we do not kiss them.' Allāh's Messenger ﷺ said, 'Can I control [the fact] that Allāh has removed mercy from your hearts.'" (*Adab al-Mufrad* 98)

Barāʾ ﵁ said, "I saw the Prophet ﷺ with Ḥasan on his shoulder. He was saying, 'O Allāh, I love him, so [you also please] love him.'" (*Adab al-Mufrad* 86)

Anas ibn Mālik ﵁ said, "A woman came to ʿĀʾishah ﵂ and ʿĀʾishah gave her three dates. The woman [then] gave each of her two children a date and kept one date for herself. The children ate the dates and then looked at their mother. She took her date and split it in two and gave each child half of the date. [Later] the Prophet ﷺ came [home] and ʿĀʾishah told him about the incident. He said, 'What amazes you about this? Allāh will show her mercy because she showed mercy to her children.'" (*Adab al-Mufrad* 89)

345 Noʿmān ibn Bashīr ﵁ related that his father [once] took him to Allāh's Messenger ﷺ, carrying him. He said, "Messenger of Allāh, I make you a witness that

Conduct with Your Relatives

Communal harmony will only be established after harmony among your relatives is developed and maintained. Even though maintaining family ties is much more challenging than maintaining friendships, you must understand that maintaining family ties is a religious obligation.[346] It is directly connected to Allāh's happiness and mercy.[347] If you strive to establish and maintain healthy relations between your relatives, you will receive Allāh's blessings throughout your life in this world and you will be compensated with Paradise in the next.[348] On the other hand if you fail to pay attention to this duty and compromise your family relations, you will suffer a tremendous loss both in this world and the next.[349]

May Allāh ﷻ protect us all. Āmīn.

I have given No'mān such-and-such [item]." The Prophet ﷺ asked, "Have you given each of your children a gift?" "No," he replied. He said, "Then make someone else a witness. [. . .] Would you not be pleased by having them all [treated with] kindness equally?" "Of course I would," he replied. The Prophet ﷺ then advised, "Then don't do what you're doing." (*Adab al-Mufrad* 92)

346 Kulayb ibn Manfa'ah reported, "My grandfather [once] asked [the Messenger ﷺ], 'Messenger of Allāh, who should I be respectful to?' The Messenger ﷺ replied, 'Your mother, your father, your sister and your brother; then your relative(s) who are connected to them. [This is a religious] right which is compulsory [upon you. It is a] family tie [that must be] kept connected.'" (*Adab al-Mufrad* 47)

347 Abū al-'Anbas ؓ related, "I visited 'Abdullāh ibn 'Amr ibn 'Ās ؓ at Waht; a plot of his in Ṭā'if. He said, 'The Prophet ﷺ pointed his finger at us and said, 'Family-ties (*raḥim*) is derived from the Most Merciful (*Raḥmān*). Whoever keeps it connected, Allāh remains connected with them, and whoever severs it, Allāh severs relations with them. *Raḥim* will have an unfettered, eloquent tongue on the Day of Rising [to contest with people in the court of Allāh].'" (*Adab al-Mufrad* 54)

348 Anas ibn Mālik ؓ reported, "Allāh's Messenger ﷺ said, 'Whoever would like their provisions to be expanded and their legacy to be prolonged, they should maintain their family-ties.'" (*Adab al-Mufrad* 56)

349 Jubayr ibn Muṭ'im ؓ reported, "I heard Allāh's Messenger ﷺ say, 'The person who severs family-ties will not enter Paradise.'" (*Adab al-Mufrad* 64)

Bibliography

Bukhārī, M. (1999) *Ṣaḥīḥ al-Bukhārī*. Riyadh, Saudi Arabia. Darussalam

———. (2003) *Adab al-Mufrad*. New Delhi, India. Maktaba al-Ilm

Ḥajjāj, M. (1998) *Ṣaḥīḥ Muslim*. Riyadh, Saudi Arabia. Darussalam

ʿĪsā, M. (1999) *Jāmiʿ al-Tirmidhī*. Riyadh, Saudi Arabia. Darussalam

Ashʿath, S. (1999) *Sunan Abū Dāwūd*. Riyadh, Saudi Arabia. Darussalam

Shuʿayb, A. (1999) *Sunan al-Nasaʾī*. Riyadh, Saudi Arabia. Darussalam

Yazīd, M. (1999) *Sunan ibn Mājah*. Riyadh, Saudi Arabia. Darussalam

Ḥākim, M. (1990) *Mustadrak ʿalā al-Ṣaḥīḥayn*. Beirut, Lebanon. Dar al-Kotob al-Ilmiyah

Bayhaqī, A.B. (1999) *Sunan al-Kubrā*. Beirut, Lebanon. Dar al-Kotob al-Ilmiyah

Haythamī, A. (2001) *Majmaʿ al-Zawāʾid*. Beirut, Lebanon. Dar al-Kotob al-Ilmiyah

Shaybānī, M. *Muʿaṭṭa li-Imām Muḥammad*. Beirut, Lebanon. Maktabah al-ʿIlmīyah

Dārquṭnī, A. (1996) *Sunan al-Dārquṭnī*. Beirut, Lebanon. Dar al-Kotob al-Ilmiyah

Kāsānī, A.B. (1997) *Badā'iʿ al-Ṣanā'iʿ fī Tartīb al-Sharā'iʿ*. Beirut, Lebanon. Dar al-Kotob al-Ilmiyah

Murghīnānī, A. *Hidāyah*. Multan, Pakistan. Maktabah Sharikah Ilmiyah

Abū Saʿīd, A. *Nūr al-Anwār*. Multan, Pakistan. Maktabah Imdādīyah

Mullā, A. I. (2004) *Kawāshif al-Jalīyah ʿan Muṣtalaḥāt al-Ḥanafīyah*. Al-Hofuf, Saudi Arabia: Maṭbaʿah al-Aḥsāʾ al-Ḥadīthah

Appendix
Traditional Kohl Products in Canada

Disclaimer: We only provide a general summary of the Canadian sources available as of 2012. For better information, please contact your local physician or your nearest Product Safety Office at 1-866-662-0666.

Sources:

- Health Concerns about Lead in Traditional Kohl *http://www.healthycanadians.gc.ca/init/cons/personal-personnels/cosmeti/kohl-info-khol-eng.php*
- Public Advisory: Traditional Kohl Products Contain Lead *http://www.hc-sc.gc.ca/ahc-asc/media/advisories-avis/_2005/2005_103-eng.php*
- Consumer Information: Health Concerns about Lead in Traditional Kohl *http://www.hc-sc.gc.ca/cps-spc/cosmet-person/cons/kohl-info-khol-eng.php*

Glossary of Arabic terms

Adhān: the first call to ritual prayer (*ṣalāh*)

Ahl al-Kitāb: People of the Book; those who follow scriptures revealed to earlier Messengers of Allāh, i.e. Jews and Christians

Ākhirah: afterlife, the hereafter, the next world

Akhlāq: moral character

Al-ḥamdu lillāh: praise be to Allāh ﷻ; an expression of gratitude

Allāh: God, the Divine

Allāhu akbar: God is the Greatest; an expression of excitement

Āmīn: an expression used to end a prayer *(duʿāʾ)*; O Allāh, please accept this prayer

Anṣārī, pl. *Anṣār*: helper; a Muslim in Madīnah who hosted the Emigrants from Makkah

As-salāmu ʿalaykum: peace be with you

As-salāmu ʿalaykum wa-raḥmatu l-lāh: peace be with you and also Allāh's mercy

As-salāmu ʿalaykum wa-raḥmatu l-lāhi wa-barakātuh: peace be with you, and also Allāh's mercy and blessings

As-salāmu ʿalaykum wa-raḥmatu l-lāhi wa-barakātuhū wa-maghfi-

ratuh: peace be with you, and also Allāh's mercy, blessings and forgiveness

Astaghfiru l-lāh: I seek Allāh's forgiveness

'Awrah: intimate parts, private parts of the body, nudity

Āyat al-Kursī: the Throne Verse (*Sūrat al-Baqarah* 2:255); Allāh's footrest[350]

Barakah: blessings; abundance of divine benefits in something

Basmalah: the phrase *bismillāhi r-raḥmāni r-raḥīm*

Buhtān: false accusation, slander

Dhikr: remembering and mentioning Allāh ﷻ

Dīn: way of life, religion

Duʿā': personal prayer, supplication; calling out to Allāh ﷻ for your needs

Dunyā: this world, worldly items

Faḍl: grace, bounty; unmerited favour of God

Faqīh, pl. *fuqahā'*: jurist; an expert in Islamic law (*fiqh*)

Fiṭrah: natural disposition

Fiqh: Islamic law; the endeavour to understand the *sharīʿah*

Furqān: the criterion or standard that separates truth from falsehood

Ghībah: backbiting, gossip

Ghusl: full ritual wash; shower or bath

Ḥadīth, pl. *aḥādīth:* narration; a traditional report of something the Prophet Muḥammad ﷺ did, said or approved of

Ḥajj: greater pilgrimage to Makkah

Ḥalāl: allowed, lawful, permissible

350 *Tafsīr al-Ṭabrī* vol.3, p.11–12

Ḥarām: not allowed, forbidden; sacred, inviolable

Hijrah: migration, e.g. of the Muslim community from Makkah to Madīnah to flee persecution

ʿĪd: festival

ʿĪd al-aḍ'ḥā: Festival of Sacrifice (10th day of the month of Dhū al-Ḥijjah)

ʿĪd al-fiṭr: Festival of Breaking Fast (1st day of the month of Shawwāl)

Imām: leader

ʿImāmah: turban

Īmān: faith; belief

In shāʾ Allāh: if Allāh ﷻ wills it; used when declaring a future action

Iqāmah: second call to prayer

Izār: lungi, sarong; a man's lower garment wrapped around the waist

Jahannam: Hell

Jāhilīyah: ignorance; not knowing about Islam; pre-Islamic period

Janābah: state of major ritual impurity

Jannah: Paradise

Jazāk Allāhu khayran: may Allāh ﷻ reward you with good

Jihād: struggle, striving, mission

Jinnī, pl. *jinn*: a type of invisible being created by Allāh ﷻ from smokeless fire; some are Muslim, some are not; they are not ghosts

Jubbah: a man's long, loose garment

Jumuʿah: gathering; congregation on Friday

Kāfir: disbeliever, faithless person, rejecter of Islam

Khalīfah: successive authority, deputy, next one in charge, trustee

Khuṭbah: address, sermon

Kufr: disbelief, ingratitude

Madh'hab, pl. *madhāhib*

Methodology

Makrūh: disliked

Mā shā' Allāh: Allāh ﷻ has willed it; an expression of joy for something good that happened or a new acquisition

Masjid, pl. *masājid*: place for *sajdah*; prayer hall, mosque

Masjid al-Ḥarām: the Sacred Mosque in Makkah

Mawlānā: our master; a title of respect for a scholar

Miswāk: natural twig toothbrush

Mu'adhdhin: muezzin; the person who calls to prayer (*ṣalāh*)

Mubārak: blessed; infused with *barakah*: *Muftī*: a scholar with the authority to issue non-binding religious rulings

Muhājir, pl. *Muhājirūn*: Emigrant; a Muslim who fled persecution in Makkah and was hosted in Madīnah

Mujāhid: warrior

Mulk: dominion, sovereignty, ultimate control

Munāfiq: hypocrite; one who pretends to be a Muslim

Nabī, pl. *Anbiyā'*: prophet; one who receives divine revelation pertaining to the *sharī'ah*: *nafl*: voluntary

Nīyah: intention

Nūr: light, radiance

Qaḍā': making up a missed ritual

Qiblah: prayer direction

Qur'ān: the Recital; the final scripture revealed to humanity after the Scrolls of Ibrāhīm ﷺ, the Torah, the Psalms and the Gospel

Rak'ah, pl. *raka'āt*: unit of prayer

Rasūl: Messenger; a prophet or angel sent by Allāh ﷻ to convey a message

Ribā: increased amount, interest, usury

Rizq: provision, sustenance; what Allāh ﷻ provides

Ṣadaqah: voluntary donation

Ṣalāh: ritual prayer; ritual worship prescribed five times a day

Salām: peace

Ṣalāt al-ʿAṣr: late afternoon prayer

Ṣalāt al-Fajr: dawn prayer

Ṣalāt al-ʿIshāʾ: night prayer

Ṣalāt al-Maghrib: sunset prayer

Ṣalāt al-Tahajjud: pre-dawn prayer

Ṣalāt al-Witr: odd-numbered prayer

Ṣalāt al-Ẓuhr: midday prayer

Ṣaḥābah: Companion; a person who saw the Prophet Muḥammad ﷺ in a state of *īmān* and died with *īmān*: *sajdah*: prostration; position of bowing face down on the ground

Ṣalawāt wa-al-taslīm: prayers and greetings of peace to the Prophet ﷺ

Ṣall Allāhu ʿalayhi wa-sallam: peace and blessings of Allāh ﷻ be upon him

Shafāʿah: intercession; pleading on another person's behalf for forgiveness or for a better result

Shām: the Levant, Greater Syria

Sharīʿah: divine code; a path of religious conduct revealed by Allāh ﷻ, the final one is defined in the Qurʾān and demonstrated in Muḥammad's legacy (*sunnah*)

Shaykh: elder, master; a title of respect for a scholar

Shayṭān, pl. *Shayāṭīn*: demon; an evil *jinnī*: *Shayṭān*: the Devil, Satan; leader of the demons (*shayāṭīn*), committed to the destruction of humanity

Subḥān Allāh: glory be to Allāh; how pure is Allāh; an expression of amazement

Sufrah: eating mat

Sunnah: generally, the legacy and tradition of the Prophet Muḥammad ﷺ; technically, an action the Prophet ﷺ practised consistently, did not abandon without a valid excuse, and did not admonish his Companions for omitting

Tafsīr: exegesis; commentary and explanation of the Qur'ān

Takbīr: the phrase *Allāhu akbar*: *taqwā*: God-consciousness, being mindful of Allāh ﷻ

Tawḥīd: Oneness of Allāh ﷻ

Ummah: community

'Umrah: lesser pilgrimage to Makkah

Tawrāt: the Torah, revealed by Allāh ﷻ to the Messenger Mūsā ﷺ

Wa-'alaykumu s-salām: and with you be peace

Waḥy: divine revelation

Wuḍū': ablutions; washing of the hands, face, forearms and feet and wiping of the head before ritual worship

Yawm al-Aḍ'ḥā: Day of Sacrifice

Yawm al-Fiṭr: Day of Breaking Fast

Zawāl: solar noon

Zinā: fornication, adultery; casual sex outside of marriage

Acknowledgements

Mathabah Publications would like to give a special thanks to the Al Nadwa Educational Islamic Centre for sponsoring a major portion of this project. It is delighting to see how our communities come together to enact Allāh's directive; "Assist each other in righteousness and being mindful [of Allāh] [. . .]."[351]

The Al Nadwa Educational Islamic Centre continuously demonstrates excellence in establishing and maintaining healthy social relations with the community at large through the programs they offer and the initiatives they undertake. We pray to Allāh that He continue to use this centre as a beacon of inspiration and enlightenment within the community until the end of time. *Āmīn*

To learn more about the Al Nadwa Educational Islamic Centre please visit http://alnadwacentre.com/.

351 *Sūrat al-Mā'idah* 5:2

Made in the USA
Monee, IL
26 August 2021

76581798R00083